GREAT
HOLIDAY
DISASTERS

GREAT HOLIDAY DISASTERS

.....and even greater travel fiascos

PERROTT PHILLIPS

CHRISTOPHER HELM
London

© 1987 Perrott Phillips
© Cartoons by Tony Husband
Christopher Helm (Publishers) Ltd, Imperial House,
21–25 North Street, Bromley, Kent BR1 1SD

British Library Cataloguing in Publication Data

Phillips, Perrott
    Great holiday disasters: — and even
    greater travel fiascos.
    1. Voyages and travels — Anecdotes,
    facetiae, satire, etc.
    I. Title
    910'.207   G465

ISBN 0–7470–2602–5

Printed and bound in Great Britain

To Irena,
who has prevented many a holiday disaster

Never Trust a Guidebook

The Fifth Earl of Cadogan summed it all up with aristocratic disdain. 'Never go abroad,' he huffed. 'It's a dreadful place.' Nobody knows whether Lord Cadogan was speaking from bitter experience, but one thing is certain: if the early guidebooks for British tourists are an accurate reflection of the trials and tribulations of foreign travel, he was only too right. Indeed, it was an understatement.

While today's guidebooks concentrate on waving palms, rolling surf and Where to Stay for Under £10 a Day, their earlier counterparts were full of dire warnings about beggars, bandits and bug-infested beds. Going to Europe on holiday or, even worse, venturing further afield, was a hazardous affair involving tearful farewells, defiantly jutting chins and mumbled words with one's executors. In fact, most guidebooks painted such an alarming picture of the perils lurking 'abroad' that it is a wonder anyone plucked up enough courage to get as far as the nearest railway station.

In probably the first real guidebook ever written – the *Codex Calixtinus*, produced around 1143 for pilgrims on the road to Santiago de Compostela – the author, Aymery Picaud, accused the northern Spaniards of poisoning the water in the wells and streams. The idea, said Picaud darkly, was to render pilgrims unconscious so that they could be murdered and robbed. Many a penitent must have dropped his watergourd in terror on reading that light-hearted piece of advice. It probably gave rise to the whole myth about 'Don't drink the water in Spain.'

Six hundred years later, things had not improved. 'Travellers should include in their luggage a machine to secure the bedchamber door at inns,' warned Philip Thicknesse in *Through France and Part of Spain*, published in 1778. 'For visitors cannot take too much caution in a country where murder and robbery are synonymous terms.'

Stuffing your luggage with items covering every conceiv-

1

able crisis or emergency was an obsession with early travel-writers. In those idyllic days, airport and dockside security checks were unheard of. Which was fortunate, as the most important thing to pack into your portmanteau was gunpowder.

According to Francis Galton's 1873 *vade-mecum*, *The Art of Travel*, gunpowder was essential for everything from curing constipation to, literally, keeping the wolf from the door. 'A glass of gunpowder in warm water is a remarkable laxative,' he claimed. Provided, of course, you didn't also enjoy a bedtime cigar.

It was when being attacked by wolves, apparently an everyday diversion east of Calais, that gunpowder really earned its luggage space. 'Put the powder in a shankbone and throw it to the pack,' he advised, presumably in all seriousness. 'When one of them gnaws and crunches it, it blows his head to atoms.' How mundane today's holiday packing sounds by comparison, with its emphasis on paperbacks by Jeffrey Archer, suntan oil and short-sleeved shirts. 'Have you remembered to pack the shankbones, darling?' strikes a far more exotic and adventurous note.

Not that there was much room to spare in Galton's time. No lily-livered nonsense then about the 44 kilos' limit, hand baggage only, and 'Can I stuff it under the aircraft seat?' For travellers embarking on the Grand Tour, a list of essentials could end up longer than the American Constitution by a couple of thousand words.

Food – that most unreliable element in foreign travel, then as now – took up most of the space in trunk, bag and valise. Nor did that mean a jar of Nescafe, a tin of baked beans and a packet of Ryvita. 'An excursion into the primeval forest of Guiana is one to be taken in all seriousness,' warned Lieutenant-colonel E. Rogers in *Advice to the Traveller*, in 1897, quelling the laughter of all those who thought a saunter round the rain forests might be a bit of a wheeze. 'Pressed food,' he continued briskly, 'bags of flour, jars of salt butter, bottles of brandy and Schiedam – with the latter's usual accompaniment of Angostura Bitters, with swizzle sticks – must be stored in the smallest space.'

The provision of iron rations like these was equally important, even if you were merely travelling by train to Paris. In his *Traveller's Manual* of 1875, Thomas Chambers admonished his readers not to unleash their lower intestine on the local cuisine, either *haute* or *basse*, until they had come to a final halt. The excitement, hurry and uncertainty of snatching meals at stations during the journey was bad for the digestive system. 'Instead,' he advised, 'you should just carry a supply of cold provisions; bread, eggs, chickens, game, sandwiches, Cornish pasties, almonds, oranges, Captain's biscuits, water and sound red wine or cold tea, sufficient to stay the appetite of the party, and let a small quantity be taken every two hours.'

However huge your hamper, you could not put off for ever the dread moment when you were forced to face your first plateful of poisonous foreign food. The thought was enough to make the stiffest British upper lip quiver, and the most formidable matriarch to reach for her *sal volatile*.

The gastronomic garbage unloaded by restaurants on unwary travellers was described by Samuel Sharp in his *Letters from Italy*. 'A soup like wash, with pieces of liver swimming in it. A plate full of brains, a dish of livers and gizzards, a turkey roasted to rags and fowls so stringy you can divide the breast into threads. The bread is bad and the butter so rancid it cannot be touched.' Apart from that, quite delicious.

Of all the abominations faced by the tourist in his search for wholesome food and drink, nothing was more noxious than Chinese champagne. The idea of a mere drop of the stuff taking the enamel off fastidious Western teeth so horrified Professor H. A. Giles that he devoted a special phrase to it in his *Chinese Without a Teacher*, in 1908. At the instant appearance of the fiendish Chinese bubbly, you simply said, '*Ch'u pa, pu yao shan-pin-chiu, na-lai yi p'ing-tzu p'i-chiu*', which meant, 'Go away. I do not wish champagne. Bring a bottle of beer. It is the English way.'

The 'English way', unfortunately, was also reflected in an air of male-chauvinist truculence which must have grated on every foreigner from Paris to Peking. The arrogant and peevish attitudes encouraged by many early British guidebooks might have accounted for the imperious manner

3

adopted by British menfolk the moment the tips of their walking sticks dug into foreign soil. Even the fastidious Dr Karl Baedeker, in his *Palestine and Syria* of 1906, advised travellers, 'The best covering for the head is an ordinary soft felt hat, a cloth cap with a visor or a pith helmet . . . the red fez should be avoided, the hat being nowadays the recognised symbol of the superior dignity of the European.'

Nor was there any effete nonsense about speaking the other fellow's language. If you failed to make yourself understood, the golden rule was to SHOUT LOUDER. 'The most important word in the Polish language, as in all others, is *Angelski*,' stated Baedeker's 1911 *Guide to Poland*. '*Angelski*, I am English, means everything.'

To be fair, consulting a phrasebook only tended to complicate matters. In his Arabic-English Dictionary, J. G. Hava gave the following definitions of the word *Khal*: 'Huge mountain. Big camel. Banner of a prince. Shroud. Fancy. Black stallion. Self-magnified. Caliphate. Lonely place, Opinion. Suspicion. Bachelor. Good manager. Horse's bit. Liberal man. Weak-bodied, weak-hearted man. Imaginative man. Free from suspicion.' A veritable minefield of misunderstanding.

For many Britons, even *Angelski* was one word too many. 'As a general rule', said one writer, with a lordly sweep of the hand, 'it should be observed that English is always understood if it is spoken clearly and accompanied by appropriate gesture or mime. His Majesty the King-Emperor is personified in every Englishman abroad and orders must be given in a suitably imperious manner. Shout if necessary. God is your authority.' Those were the days.

When all else failed, a sharp whack across the shoulders with Milord's Malacca cane worked wonders. 'However,' conceded Francis Galton, 'a young traveller must be discriminating and cautious in the licence he allows his stick.'

Tourism itself was, in a sense, a Great Travel Disaster. For deep down and without a glimmering of self-doubt, every Englishman (and some Englishwomen) knew that foreigners

4

were somehow . . . well . . . *inferior*. 'The lower classes in Florence are in general ill-looking,' sniffed Anna Jameson in her *Traveller's Diary* of 1826, while Thomas Nugent in *The Grand Tour* dismissed the French as 'being little better than hypocrites in their cringes and impertinent ceremonies'.

The loose morals of foreigners represented a constant threat to blushing English maidenhood, even when under strict surveillance. 'All men who have young and beautiful wives should avoid a trip to Paris,' cautioned Philip Thicknesse. 'She must be good and wise, too, if six weeks does not corrupt her mind and debauch her morals.'

Protecting one's wife from the advances of lecherous foreigners was only half the problem. If they weren't after your wife, they were after your wallet. The remainder were too stupid to appreciate either, but still possessed considerable nuisance value.

'When collecting letters from a poste restante, check under the letter E,' advised Richard Ford in his 1855 *Handbook for Travellers in Spain*. 'The Spaniards have difficulty in understanding English and American names and they are perplexed by our custom of ending a person's name with the word Esquire. As a result, many letters get filed away under E.'

Sending back his picture postcards – 'Having a dreadful time. Be grateful you're not here' – had clearly been a traumatic experience for Ford. 'Never trust a casual servant to post your correspondence,' he wrote. 'They can rarely resist the temptation of destroying the letters and charging you for the postage.' Nor was that the worst of it. 'As private letters are opened with very little scruple in Spain', he added, 'correspondents should be cautious, especially in political subjects.'

Having made sure your message was sufficiently innocuous – and rejected the offers of light-fingered messengers – the walk to the post office could prove the most dangerous part of the whole enterprise. A visitor who merely wanted to say 'Plenty of sun, food wonderful' was often lucky to get back to his hotel in one piece. For a start, there were the beggars. 'They are the plague of Spain,' trembled Ford.

'They have a knack of finding out a stranger and worrying him and bleeding him as effectually as mosquitoes. The regular form of uncharitable rejection is "My brother, will

you excuse me for God's sake?''. If this request be gravely
said, the mendicant gives up hope of copper. Any other
answer only encourages importunity, as the beggars do not
believe in the reality of the refusal and therefore never leave
off until, in despair, you give them hush-money to silence
their whine.'

It was when the whine of the beggars was drowned by the
whine of bullets that it was best to throw your letters to the
wind and take to your heels. 'On passing soldiers on duty',
continued Ford, keeping his head well down, 'remember that
the challenge of a Spanish sentry is *Quien vive?* The answer
is *España*. Then follows *Quien gente?* The answer is *Paisano*.
The sooner and quicker strangers answer, the better, as
silence arouses suspicion and in Spain a shot often precedes
any explanation.'

Cheated by rapacious beggars, robbed of your stamp
money by rascally servants, in trouble with the secret police
and winged by the bullets of trigger-happy sentries, you
stagger to the doctor to be patched and pampered. A fatal
move.

'Both your life and your purse are in danger with a Spanish
doctor,' grumbled Ford. For modest young ladies, the ordeal
was doubly embarrassing. 'The most intimate details of the
anatomy are required in dealing with foreign physicians,'
noted a scandalised *Cook's Tourist Guide* in 1899. ' ''Please, a
plaster to relieve the pain caused by falling on my cocyx''
would be unthinkable at home but *de rigueur* abroad.'

Men, of course, were made of sterner stuff and could face
with equanimity the spectre that still haunts foreign travel to
this very day . . . the hotel which looks so inviting on the
holiday brochure, but which turns out to be still in the
cement-mixer.

As usual, the indefatigable Galton provided the answer.
'Any European can live through a bitter night on a perfectly
dry sandy plain without any clothes beside what he has on',

he assured his readers, 'if he buries his body pretty deeply in the same, keeping his head above ground.'

The only snag with this novel method of getting a free night's accommodation, with eye-level view of the beach, was the risk of being surprised by unfriendly natives still smarting from some Great White Tourist's Malacca cane. This probably explains why, in 1890, 'A Gentleman of Experience' urged travellers to learn the various African versions of the phrase, 'I am an Englishman and require instant attention to the damage done to my solar topee.' Travel may broaden the mind. But it can be harder on the pith helmet, particularly when the natives start hitting back.

The word 'travel', you will not be astonished to learn, stems from the French word *travail*, which meant (and still means) 'bodily or mental labour or toil, especially of a painful or oppressive nature; exertion; trouble; hardship; suffering'. The whole concept of tourism may have changed immeasurably since the Earl of Cadogan's day, but, as this book proves, the message remains the same: sometimes it is better to travel hopefully than to arrive.

When in Rome

Nobody set off more hopefully than Mr Nicholas Scotti, of San Francisco. In 1977, Mr Scotti, who speaks very little English, kissed his family goodbye and flew from America to his native Italy to visit relatives. On the way, his plane made an unscheduled stop at Kennedy Airport. Convinced that he had arrived, Mr Scotti got out and spent two disconcerting days in New York believing all the time he was in Rome. Assuming the relatives who had agreed to meet him had been delayed, he set out to track down their address. As luck would have it, many of the New Yorkers he bumped into were of Italian descent and spoke the language. One was a Naples-born policeman who put him on a bus bound for the city's large Italian quarter. Twelve hours and several bus rides later, Mr Scotti was handed over by a bewildered driver to another policeman, who spoke no Italian. After a brief argument, during which Mr Scotti expressed amazement that the Rome police employed officers who couldn't even speak their own language, it was gently explained to him that he was in New York. He refused to believe it. As a police car raced him back to the airport with sirens wailing, Scotti was still unconvinced. 'Only the Italians drive like this,' he insisted. The one mystery, he confessed later, was the disappearance of some of Rome's famous landmarks. 'Whatever happened to the Colosseum?' he complained.

Flight of Fancy

Airports are confusing at the best of times, so Mr and Mrs Evans, of Staines, in Middlesex, thought they had done quite well to get on board the plane to Palma, Majorca, without a hitch, particularly as it was their first holiday abroad. Halfway through the flight, however, a double check by cabin staff revealed they were on the wrong plane, at the wrong time, going to the wrong place. Mr and Mrs Evans had religiously followed all the announcements at Gatwick Airport for the Palma flight, because that was the name of the hotel they had chosen for their package holiday. Unfortunately, the Hotel Palma was in Benidorm.

On Vacation

Edward and Maureen Bell, from Doncaster, got the right plane, and even ended up at the right hotel, at Torremolinos, on Spain's Costa del Sol. However, they made one small mistake. They misread the 'Departing guests' notice on the

back of the bedroom door. Every day for a fortnight, they vacated their room by 12 o'clock, baggage and all, unpacking all over again each evening when they returned from the beach. 'It seemed a bit odd at the time,' they admitted.

Transitory Pleasure

Strangeways, in Manchester, is, notoriously, Britain's most depressing and overcrowded prison. The only light relief is provided by the bus which whisks inmates to and from the gloomy Victorian building. Along its side are the words, 'Smith's Happiways Tours'.

Railroaded

Sefton Delmer, the legendary foreign correspondent of the pre-war *Daily Express*, once took a holiday in the United States, travelling coast to coast by rail. On the third morning, his composure was somewhat ruffled when he found he was sharing his sleeping compartment with a large and manifestly well-fed bedbug. At the first convenient stop, Delmer dashed off a furious letter to the railroad company, threatening legal action unless he received full compensation. The result was probably the most grovelling letter of apology ever composed. The company was mortified at the incident. 'Never in the history of this railroad has such an appalling thing ever occurred,' Delmer was assured. 'We adopt the highest standards of inspection, maintenance and hygiene,' it went on, 'and we can assure you that no effort is being spared to discover how this unfortunate incident could possibly have happened.' After another full page of anguished contrition, the letter ended with an open invitation for Delmer to travel any time, anywhere, on the railroad free of charge, plus a full refund of his fare. Delmer was feeling rather pleased with himself when he noticed a small slip of paper inside the envelope, which had obviously been left in by mistake. On it were scribbled the words, 'Give this bum the bug letter.'

Swimming in Oil and Reeking of Garlic

The package-tour holidaymakers had just arrived in Paris and were enjoying their first meal in the hotel dining room.

All, that is, except a woman in a florid dress who was becoming increasingly agitated. Finally, she got up and went over to the courier. 'It's the olive oil,' she said, quivering with the kind of moral indignation the British usually reserve for evidence of moral turpitude among the natives. 'You've got to do something about it. It's upsetting my Albert.' She motioned imperiously at her husband, who was sitting wan and motionless at the table.

Perplexed, as nobody had complained about the olive oil before, the courier went to the manager. 'Olive oil!' the manager exploded, throwing in a few highly spiced Gallic imprecations for good measure. 'Now look. I learned all about the British and olive oil fifteen years ago. I use sunflower oil for cooking, I use lard, butter, how-you-say *dripping*, but never a drop of olive oil!'

The courier crept back to the table, where the couple were still waiting grimly for satisfaction, and started to explain to them that they were mistaken about the olive oil in the food. The woman cut him short. 'We weren't complaining that they use it on the food,' she said. 'It's just that there is a cruet of it on the table and the very sight of it makes my Albert ill.'

If, God forbid, any of you are thinking of going abroad and opening up a little hotel or restaurant for British tourists, let that be a lesson to you. The average Briton on holiday will put up with anything – delayed planes, unfinished hotels, lost luggage, lumpy beds, punitive customs officials and grumpy policemen – but there is one thing that will bring out the beast in him in a flash. Funny Foreign Food.

Travel-writer Jackie Smith was once deputed to accompany an elderly British couple on a weekend trip to Calais, a prize they had won in a magazine competition. Just before they boarded the ferry, the wife turned to Jackie and, in what must be the gastronomic *non sequitur* of all time, said 'My husband's terribly choosy about his food. He won't touch any of that French stuff.'

The great Mediterranean tourist playground may be the

place where cafes proudly proclaim 'Tea as Mum makes it –
we warm the pot first', but, for many British visitors, far
worse horrors lurk behind those swinging kitchen doors than
the occasional teabag. Garlic, for example. A tourist in Catto-
lica actually demanded to see the British Consul after finding
a clove of the dreaded bulb in his salad.

That was nothing, however, compared to the Great Rabbit
Riot, which almost threatened to wreck Anglo-Spanish
relations for ever. It was at the time when the myxomatosis
plague was sweeping through Britain, killing every bunny in
its path. The disease was quite unknown in Majorca and one
hotel catering for package tourists decided to serve *Lapin
Chasseur* for the main meal.

The moment the first plateful of rabbit appeared, there
was uproar. One of the diners rushed round the restaurant
exhibiting the noxious meal and within minutes an angry
mob was battering on the manager's door, demanding an
explanation. Wisely, he locked himself in, so the protesters,
still holding aloft the rapidly congealing plate of rabbit, peas
and potatoes, piled into a fleet of taxis and made for the
Town Hall. Somehow, they forced their way into the office
of the Commissioner of Public Works, who couldn't speak a
word of English but knew a hysterical mob when he saw
one. The man went ashen with terror as the offending plate

12

was shoved under his nose and a dozen angry fingers threatened him.

It was at this climactic moment that the group's courier, a conscientious and intelligent girl, caught up with them on her bicycle. What happened then has become a legend among travel representatives throughout the Balearics. With contemptuous aplomb, the girl lifted the rabbit leg between her fingers and nibbled the bone clean. Then she tossed it over her shoulder like Charles Laughton in *Henry VIII*, mounted her bicycle and pedalled to the post office, where she cabled her immediate resignation.

On holiday, I like to remain as inconspicuous as possible. But it was the memory of the Great Rabbit Riot that impelled me to avert a similar fracas in Benidorm.

The first sounds of mutiny were heard when the waiters started serving globe artichokes. To the chef, it must have seemed like an inspired idea. Artichokes had been particularly cheap in the market that day, and there had been comments about the monotony of the menu. How was he to know that not a single person in the dining room had seen an artichoke in captivity before? The first aggressive voice rang clearly across the room, 'I'm not eating this. It's a cactus!' While others pushed and prodded the mysterious object with their forks, one man proudly offered the solution, 'It's some sort of pot plant,' and put it in his pocket, presumably to replant it in John Innes No. 1 when he returned home.

As the vague mumble of discontent rose, an awful vision struck me of scenes at the town hall, strained diplomatic relations, chilly notes between the Foreign Office and the Spanish Embassy and renewed argument over Gibraltar. Oilier than the sauce vinaigrette, I oozed toothily from table to table, demonstrating how the vegetable should be eaten. It was merely a qualified success. Nearly 200 of the 220 artichokes went back to the kitchen uneaten, but at least I can claim to have avoided adding the ignominy of Artichoke Anarchy to the Great Rabbit Riot.

The British are a strange and contrary people, and Funny Foreign Food can sometimes be absorbed happily if taken out of the context of cuisine. If, for example, it can be relegated to the level of sport, then you are on to a winner.

Travel courier Tom Crichton remembers with a chill the shocked silence that greeted the appearance of *escargots* in a Provençal cafe to which he had taken his party after an excursion. Luckily, one of the group had been hitting the *ordinaire* with almost suicidal abandon during the day, and with a whoop of 'Let's see who can eat the most!', descended on them with a flailing fork. Not to be outdone, several others took up the challenge and soon the fastest snail race ever known was in progress. Completely forgetting their earlier revulsion, everyone joined in. The instigator of the contest won with a stomach-boggling total of nearly 100.

Some of that pioneering, competitive spirit would not have come amiss at the hotel I stayed at in Torremolinos, the Miami Beach of southern Spain, which was packed with British tourists of the most reactionary kind. Imagine my surprise when one of the guests, who had clearly read a guidebook or two, asked the head waiter if he could order *paella* for his family the following evening. The waiter was equally stunned at this completely unexpected request for southern Spain's most *tipico* dish; steaming saffron rice stuffed with chicken and multi-coloured shellfish and decorated with red and green peppers.

The Spanish rose to the occasion magnificently. The following evening, the head waiter himself proudly led a colourful procession from the kitchen, as the superb *paella*, in a huge iron dish, was borne in by waiters in white shirts, red sashes and what appeared to be flamenco dancers' trousers. It was a moving sight and for a moment I felt ashamed that I had so misjudged my fellow guests.

But even as the procession stopped at the family's table, I had an overwhelming premonition of disaster. 'Just a minute,' said one of the group, as the waiter was about to ladle out the *paella*. Producing an Instamatic camera, he

14

quickly took a flashlight picture of the waiter and the exuber-
antly displayed food; then his wife with waiter and *paella;*
then his wife and children with waiter and *paella.* Handing
the camera to his wife, he posed for a final picture of himself,
children, waiter and *paella.* The awful moment had come. He
put the camera away, turned to the head waiter and said,
'Thanks. I only wanted it for the photos. We'll carry on with
the set meal now, thank you.'

I have seen the same expression on the faces of bullfighters
as the *muleta* is snatched from their hands by a violent bull,
in the eyes of El Greco saints going to their martyrdom, on
the faces of the men before the firing squad in Goya's picture
'*May 3rd 1808*', but I never thought I would see it engraved
on the features of a team of waiters in a tourist hotel in
Torremolinos.

To be fair, international restaurateurs often make things
difficult for their guests, once they launch into what they
think is the English language. Maybe it is revenge for gener-
ations of 'No speaka your lingo' British visitors.

Arthur Eperon, author of many travel books, once saw a
party of British tourists stop dead in their tracks outside a
Spanish restaurant. From the expressions on their faces it
was clear that all their worst suspicions about Continental
decadence had been confirmed. Fathers bristled angrily and
mothers covered their children's eyes. 'Disgusting!'
exclaimed one woman with all the righteous indignation that
only the misinformed can command. In huge letters a notice
proclaimed the restaurant's speciality of the day, 'Rape,
seamanlike style'. As they all took to their heels, it was too
late for anyone to explain that only the British language had
been seriously assaulted. It was just the chef's garbled way
of translating the popular Spanish dish, *rape marinero*, or
angler-fish in a white wine sauce.

The menu item 'Tart of the House, 1 franc' has long since
gone down into gastronomic folklore (along with the one
franc). Yet a list of dishes offered recently by a restaurant in
Albufeira, Portugal, would have made the most adventurous

eater-out take one look, drop his napkin and flee. Among the delicacies were 'Friend flounder, Assaulted artichokes, Eggs good woman, Bee tongue friend, Bluberlips and Gread meet rollis'.

Given an English dictionary with half the pages missing, a typewriter that jams every fourth letter and a chronic attack of dyslexia, a really dedicated restaurateur can make the most ordinary dishes sound alarming, if not actually homicidal.

It is safe to assume that the 'horse-rubbish sauce' advertised in a restaurant in Rome meant horse-radish sauce, since the alternative doesn't bear thinking about. And it is not too difficult to translate 'Roast cow and smashed potos' in Malaga, 'Fright chicken' in Golden Sands, Bulgaria, and 'Swine slice' in Bremen. But what nightmare ingredients go into 'Boiled combinations' in Singapore, 'Game and spit' on the Greek island of Kos, 'Smoked couch' in Alicante, 'Utmost of chicken blight' in Lido di Jesolo and the diabolical 'Dried horse's been' offered at a taverna in Piraeus Harbour, Greece?

'We always serve tea in a Bag like mother,' assured a cafe in Las Palmas, while another in the Costa Brava tempted diners of more robust tastes with 'Giant Highlander Sandwich'. The Giant Highlandburger might have proved as tough as the 'Beef Strongenuff' featured by a hotel dining room in Bangkok, which went on to dangle even more exotic culinary delights in 'Wedding soup, Grilled lamp, Fried gut Siam-style, Stewed abalone with 3 things and Lucky duck.'

There is an awful air of finality about the 'Terminal soup' offered by the restaurant in Istanbul Airport. And more than a hint of sadism in the 'Torture Soup' and 'Grilled Tender Lion' on the menu of the El Jahra Restaurant, in Djerba. However, it takes a finer mind than mine to unravel the menu at a restaurant in Penang which presents a complete range of incomprehensible dishes, including 'Egg fiemush, Srips, Stripe omelette, Bee tongue fred and Gibeless tree ice flawn'.

Mr Norman Hammond, archeological correspondent of *The Times*, dug up an extraordinary menu at the Sitara Restaurant in New York, which offered '5 Apron Rice, Crab Meat Shaag and Botty Kebab'. This archeological find prompted *The Times* to invite its readers to submit further examples. Actor Derek Nimmo came up with 'Claypot with Eight Fairies' from Bangkok; J. R. E. Adams recommended a restaurant in Barcelona serving 'Guts, Slap sepia, Slamns, Shails and Squit to the Romana'; from Naxos, T. H. Leibowitz culled 'Lamb cook to a Peasant and Small Try' and the Rev. Ivor Scott-Oldfield brought back 'Farte aux fraises' from the menu of the Turkish ship, *Karadeniz*. Lady Kinloss stumbled on the disturbingly cannibalistic 'Fried Brian' in Granada, Dr. C. D. V. Wilson reported seeing 'Kidneys of the chef' in Geneva and from Honduras, Norman Thomas produced 'Chap suey'.

Sometimes, these mistranslations achieve an eccentric logic of their own, like the Madrid restaurant which defined *gazpacho* as 'Frozen soap with peccadilloes', or the pricey bistro at Bresse where *quenelles de brochet à la Nantua* ended up uncomfortably as 'Pike balls at the Nantua'.

However, I still do not know whether the imperative 'Up

egg with peases!' at a restaurant in Oporto was some delicious Portuguese speciality or yet another revolutionary rallying-cry. Nor did I stop to find out.

With restaurants all over the world providing these mystery tours through the lower intestine, it is no wonder that the tariff in a cafeteria in Dubrovnik, Yugoslavia, ends with the defiant note, 'If you are satisfactory, tell your friends. If you are unsatisfactory, warn the waitress'.

No amount of warning, one feels, would shed any useful light on Slap Sepia or Gibeless tree ice flawn. Yet despite mounting frustration (not to speak of nausea), one cannot help feeling sorry for the cafe-owner in Tenerife who, after patient experiment with the right combination of whiskey, black coffee and cream, proudly introduced Gaelic Coffee into his menu. Unfortunately, he typed the letter 'r' instead of 'e' and in one stroke invented a concoction so fiendish that it almost takes one's breath away. It came out as 'Garlic Coffee'.

Time Off

American tourists tend to get bemused by the sheer time-span of European recorded history. A British Tourist Association guide who took a party of Americans to Runnymede decided to explain all about King John and the Magna Carta. He only got as far as the words, 'This is where Magna Carta was signed . . .' when a deep transatlantic voice interrupted, 'Say, when was that?' Without a pause the courier replied, '1215.' 'Darn it,' said the tourist, looking at his watch, 'we've missed it by twenty minutes!'

Venetian Blind

On their way back from a trip to Rome in 1950, during Holy
Year, a group of Galway county councillors stopped over at
Venice. They were so taken with the city that at the next
council meeting it was proposed that they should buy a
gondola as a tourist attraction for Lough Corrib. The motion
was seconded by one of the councillors who had not been
on the trip, and who was not quite sure what a gondola was.
He added an amendment that they order two gondolas – one
male and one female – so that they could mate and, hopefully, breed.

Trunk in Charge

It just wasn't Antonio's day – although it seemed to start
perfectly, with Antonio Jiminez taking delivery of his new
car after waiting five months. Puffed up with 'pride of owner-
ship', as the car advertisements say, he surveyed his
£7,000–worth of sparkling bodywork and told his wife, 'Hop
in! We're going for a spin to the new safari park down the
road.' The total shambles that followed was recounted in the
Spanish magazine, *Lookout*.

Like many southern Spaniards, Antonio was an amiable
know-all. You couldn't tell him anything. So when his wife
and two children rolled into the safari park, near his home
at La Linea, on the southern coast, Antonio immediately
started a long lecture on the subject of Life in the Wild.
'Wind down your window so you can get a better look at
the animals,' he told his wife. 'Dangerous? Nonsense. Wild

animals have never been known to attack people in their cars.'

At that moment, the huge trunk of an elephant snaked in through the passenger window and fastened itself round Senora Jiminez's neck. Instead of driving away, Antonio reached across and angrily wound up the window, trapping the trunk inside. With a roar of pain, the elephant pulled out his trunk and furiously stamped on the car, denting it from boot to bonnet.

Hysterical, the family screamed to Antonio, 'Get us out of here!' But Antonio knew his rights. 'Not until I get compensation,' he shouted back.

Nursing his radically modified vehicle back to the entrance, Antonio leaped out and demanded to see the proprietor. 'What are you going to do about it?' he said, pointing dramatically at the crumpled car. Patiently, the proprietor told him he had violated the park rules by rolling down his window and therefore had no right to any compensation. 'I'll tell you what,' he offered. 'Have a large brandy to settle your nerves, with our compliments.' Reluctantly, and with some ill grace, Antonio downed a couple of large ones and drove off home, breathing both vengeance and brandy fumes.

He was nearly at his front door when he saw an accident,

ZE ONLY ELEPHANTs YOU'VE ENCOUNTERED MY FRIEND ARE PINK ONES

and pulled up to help. He was still interfering when the police arrived, took one look at his restructured car and assumed he had been involved in the crash. 'No, no,' said Antonio impatiently, as the policeman took out his notebook, 'an elephant jumped on it.'

The policeman had seen most things, but never an elephant on the main road to La Linea. Then he caught a whiff of Antonio's breath. Whipping out a breathalyser-bag, the policeman ordered Antonio to blow into it, whereupon the brandies did their stuff and the crystals turned a pretty shade of green. Antonio was booked for drunken driving and ordered to take his family home by bus.

No, it certainly wasn't his day. Next day wasn't much better, either. He got a vet's bill from the safari park . . . for treatment of the elephant's injured trunk.

One Lump or Two?

On holiday in India, Mr John Willson, of East Dereham, Norfolk, met a smart, well-spoken Indian on the bus to Indore. They chatted amiably for two hours and when they had to change buses at Bhopal, the Indian offered to buy him a tea. Mr Willson remembered only the first ten minutes of the bus journey from Bhopal. He next awoke in hospital in Indore, having been taken unconscious from the bus by two policemen who thought he was drunk. When he went back to check his belongings at the police station, Mr Willson discovered that he had been stripped of his money-belt, containing travellers' cheques and cash, two cameras and lenses, and his passport. In addition to pickpockets and bag-snatchers, the police explained, there was now a new type of criminal to beware of: robbers who slipped drugs into the tea of unsuspecting Western tourists. Mr Willson had been tea-mugged.

All the Fun of the Fiasco

Judging by the leaflet thrust into my hands, the fiesta was going to be the biggest thing to hit Spain since the Moors arrived on the first 'package tour' in 711. Even taking into account conventional Spanish hyperbole, the ultimate in drama, spectacle and excitement was about to be unleashed on the village:

> Grand Regatta and procession across the bay by magnificently decorated boats! Thrilling boat race with a superb prize for the winner! Great tug of war between adults and children! Stupendous display of fireworks! Extraordinary cavalcade of vintage vehicles with passengers in period costume! Wonderful launching of balloons with prizes! Great and spectacular final carnival with election of Beauty Queen!

All that was before total chaos set in. From the word go, there appeared to be no co-operation at all between the organisers of the various events, who treated each other with the deepest suspicion. I got the distinct impression that none of them had been on speaking terms since the last fiesta.

The first the local Mayor heard about the cavalcade of cars – borrowed from the collection of a wealthy Briton living nearby in gin-soaked retirement – was when he read it in the handbill. Miffed at not being consulted, he banned the parade and declared publicly, 'If those old cars come in here, I'll punch the leader on the nose!'

After much heated discussion, a compromise was reached by allowing a few of the cars to drive quickly in and out of the village on another day. Naturally, nobody informed anyone of the change of plan, with the result that bewildered people in period costume were left roaming the streets on the advertised day, vainly trying to link up with the procession. One eccentric came down from the hills in a decorated horse-cart, with his brother dressed as a woman and twirling a parasol. They returned, highly disgruntled, with the jeers of the crowd ringing in their ears.

The Grand Regatta consisted of five fishing smacks furtively sneaking across the harbour as if on a smuggling expedition, and only four rowing-boats competed in the 'Thrilling boat race'. One failed to start, the second sprang a leak halfway, the third lost its oars and the winner's 'Superb prize' turned out to be an outsized bun.

The children who lost the tug of war burst into tears and when a local cafe-owner promised to pacify all the losers with free lemonade, he found that the team had mysteriously multiplied by the time it reached his shop. He was last seen gnashing his teeth and opening the forty-fifth bottle.

Something went wrong with the gas cylinders and the balloons shot into the air, never to be seen again. The first fireworks failed to go off and, when they were replaced by highly explosive fog maroons, the crowd scattered in terror.

As if all this was not enough, the beauty queen's crown was won by a French girl – the daughter of a visitor – who was soundly booed by loyal locals who had placed their money on Lola from the fruit market.

The whole affair was an utter shambles, everyone had a wonderful time, and it all happened in a fishing village only an olive-stone's throw from one of the most tourist-infested beaches in Majorca.

Thanks to television, everyone is familiar with the big celebrations which set cities like Jerez, Seville and Pamplona on their ears for weeks at a time. British tourists pour in by the coachload; and generally have to be poured out again the other end. But the ones you don't read about in the Spanish National Tourist Office's publicity handouts are the gimcrack little village affairs where fiesta turns into fiasco before you can say *Olé!*

A fiesta at Nerja, on the Costa del Sol, some years ago was conducted in an atmosphere of feud, enmity and suspicion that would have brought a smile of recognition to the faces of the Borgias. It all started when the Town Hall increased the price of admission to the events in the official marquee. Overnight, the streets of the village erupted in a nasty rash of posters printed by the local Communist Party, accusing the Town Hall of running the fiesta for the benefit of bloated officials, hangers-on and freeloaders. 'How many free passes are handed out to town hall stuffed-shirts and their cronies?' the Reds wanted to know.

The following day the reason for the increased prices became apparent. Some of the biggest names in Spanish show business had been booked to appear at the marquee. The Town Hall had also published a lavish 'Guide to the Fiesta' which somehow had to be paid for. The authorities had, as they say, 'gone over the top'.

Now the recriminations started in earnest. The Ratepayers' Association got together and demanded 'a fiesta by the people, for the people'. The Independence for Andalusia Party wanted to know why they had to import 'foreigners from Madrid' to entertain the townsfolk. 'Have we not got talent of our own right here?' they wanted to know, a question which was answered by an immediate and overwhelming surge of silence.

The climax came when the Communist Party somehow got hold of a list of free passholders and, with a cackle of self-righteous glee, distributed copies in the streets. 'Parasites on the body of the working class!' cried one devout party member melodramatically as he thrust the damning document into my hand.

Even the most optimistic reveller had to agree it was not the most auspicious beginning to the fiesta. One group of German tourists never even recovered from the opening ceremony, when fishermen wandered through the streets at six in the morning, letting off extremely dangerous-looking distress rockets. At the first explosion, the Germans rushed on to their balconies, shouting 'Basque bombs!' Then they packed their bags and fled.

A similar, if slightly more delayed, shock was in store for the thirty Britons who had booked into the village's only smart hotel, wreathed by palms in a corner of the town where barely the squeak of a *cicada* disturbed the calm. For a mere £400 for the fortnight, they had arrived, as the London tour-operator's brochure put it, 'to relax in a quiet and unspoiled corner of the coast, far from the tourist crowds.' How were they, or the company, to know that, once a year, the elegant area outside the hotel became the fiesta fairground. Spanish fairgrounds do not merely whirl away merrily into the small hours. They are also DEAFENING. Far into the early morning, the distraught British, in their Marks & Sparks pyjamas, nighties and dressing-gowns, could be seen gathered on their balconies. Spotlit in the garish neon of the fairground, they looked like angry little puppets, their arms waving furiously and their desperate cries swallowed up in the excruciating din.

Having made their point, the Communists retreated to their own marquee where, by common consent, they served the best barbecued chicken in the fiesta. 'You can tell it's a communist chicken,' observed a local wit, 'because it has two left wings.'

All the fun of the fiasco seemed to be over, so I went off to join the celebrations at another village further up the coast. I was not disappointed.

The local priest had announced that the annual ceremony of 'Blessing the Animals' would take place on the church steps. No doubt it seemed a good idea at the time. But the villagers, augmented by curious tourists, arrived in their hundreds, turning the square into one vast menagerie. Farmers struggled to control bullocks, cows, flocks of chickens, goats and gaggles of geese. Villagers carrying turkeys, caged birds, lambs, cats, dogs and piglets fought to get near the church steps, where the priest stood intoning his blessing and flicking Holy Water at any of God's creatures within range.

Things started going irreversibly wrong when a horseman appeared with a frisky white stallion. One flick of the water was enough. The beast took fright and kicked out, knocking over a donkey cart and a woman carrying a cockerel. This terrified some chickens which scattered across the road into a group waiting with domestic pets. In a few moments it was bedlam, with snorts, howls, clucks, barks and whinnies punctuated by the shouting of angry spectators as creatures of every kind bolted and panicked among the crowd. Amid all this, apparently oblivious to the pandemonium, the priest unconcernedly carried on, blessing every animal and distracted owner who flashed past, and flicking the Holy Water after them.

If you look hard enough, I concluded with some satisfaction, you can always find a fiasco.

Throwing in the Towel

The quickest way to re-fight World War Two, or even lay the foundations of World War Three, is to put British and German holidaymakers in the same hotel; and nothing is calculated to lead to hostilities quicker than the vexed question of Who Bags the Sun-loungers First.

Anglo-German tempers were getting very frayed round a hotel swimming-pool on the Algarve coast, in Portugal. It was basically the fault of the large German contingent, who elected one of their number to go round the pool at five o'clock each morning, laying out the sun-mattresses for all the others. By the time the British emerged from breakfast, all the best places had been 'taken', even though most of the Germans were still munching through their Spiegelei-und-Speck. One British holidaymaker finally rebelled. Waiting until the mattress-Führer had done his rounds, he wandered over to the sunniest spot and replaced an 'enemy' mattress with his own; worse still, he 'interned' the captured mattress in his room on the ground floor. War had formally been declared. Every day the furious German whose foxhole had been mopped up pressed his nose against the Briton's window, pointed to the imprisoned mattress and shook his fist.

It was on the last day of the German's holiday, after he had thrown a dreadful fit and threatened to break down the Briton's door, that the courier stepped in as peacemaker. And not a moment too soon. Gently, the courier broke the news to Our Hero. The poor German had been livid for good reason. It was his own mattress. He had brought it all the way from Bremen, and now he wanted it back before he flew off.

Getting the Bird

The brightly coloured Javanese sparrow hopped along the pack of cards spread out in front of him . . . hesitated . . . then suddenly started pecking at one. The aged fortune-teller sitting in the village square removed the card, then turned to the customer who was waiting to see what Fate had up its sleeve. 'You will travel far. See many strange sights. Meet many people,' he intoned. 'But do not travel by boat. It is written in the cards!'

It is the kind of scene that would bring a smile to the face of the most dyspeptic television producer; and, indeed, so it did. A Thames Television team had been combing Hong Kong for locations for their holiday programme, *Wish You Were Here?* In a willow-pattern village, they had stumbled on

a Chinese fortune-teller practising the ancient art of ornithomancy – using birds to predict the future.

They arranged with the fortune-teller to film him and his psychic sparrow at work the next day, with presenter Judith Chalmers as the 'customer'. 'He is one hundred per cent good fortune-teller feller,' confirmed the Chinese interpreter. 'He sit there every day for years. Never wrong. He sees into future.' But there was something the little bird hadn't told him.

The next day the team returned to the village, weighed down with cameras, lighting equipment, miles of cable, tape-recorders – everything except the studio sink. Judith wore a scarlet-silk *cheongsam* and had memorised her lines in the script. The only thing missing was the fortune-teller.

After a rapid conversation with one of the villagers, the interpreter turned to the scriptwriter with an anguished look. 'Tellible news!' he said. 'The fortune-teller isn't coming.'

'For God's sake, why not?'

'He is in mourning.'

'Who has died?'

'The bird.'

Return Booking

If you are ever mugged, robbed or cheated in Istanbul, it might be a good idea to book in immediately at the Motel Antalya, on Turkey's Mediterranean coast. 'Things that were taken away from you in the restless cities', claims the hotel brochure, 'will be given back to you at this fine motel.'

Missing the Boat

For nearly twenty years, a distinguished editorial executive on the London *Evening News* took regular day-trips to Boulogne on the cross-Channel ferry. Strangely, the only part he ever remembered was the voyage out. It was the *vin rouge* that did it. Ernie used to get so much down that, by the evening, he was in no position to tell a ferryboat from a four-in-hand.

Luckily, he had made friends with the Boulogne *gendarmerie*. They had strict orders to pick him up ten minutes before the boat sailed (he was a conspicuously rotund character) and, despite any struggle or protest, get him aboard on time. 'However desperately I plead to stay', Ernie told them soberly, 'it is only the drink talking. Ignore me. Just pour me on to the ferry.'

It worked like a charm. He never missed the last boat home, even though his own legs never got him up the gangplank – until he decided to take his wife on a two-week motoring holiday through France. Their first night's stop was Boulogne and, around seven in the evening, Ernie got the taste. 'You don't mind if I pop out and have a couple of drinks?' he asked his wife. 'I'll be back in an hour.'

Two drinks led to three, then four. A couple of hours later, he was past caring. At that point, the *gendarmerie* looked into the cafe, saw him in his usual transcendental state, checked with their watches and exclaimed, 'Alors! Ze ferryboat! Vite!'

It was no use protesting that he was on the first night of a holiday. He was frogmarched cheerfully to the ferry and dumped on board only seconds before it sailed.

The following morning, his distraught wife got a telegram from him from Dover. 'Oh well,' it said, 'let's try again.'

Light Fantastic

That prince among pianists, the late Artur Rubinstein, told this wonderful story of his first visit to Russia since the end of World War Two. Checking into his hotel in Moscow, he became gradually obsessed with the idea that the room might be bugged. Many old and politically out-of-favour friends had promised to visit him, and it was only fair to them to take every possible precaution. Rubinstein checked behind pictures, along the picture rails, under the furniture, inside the vases and lampshades, but found nothing. By midnight, he had covered the entire room, still without any success. It was only when he finally crawled between the sheets that the idea hit him: Under the bed! And there it was, four crossed copper wires fed into a recess in the floorboards beneath the carpet. Silently, so as not to alert the eavesdroppers, Rubinstein got out his nail file and gently sawed through the wires until they disappeared from view. When he came down the following morning, Rubinstein spotted the manager in the foyer and cheerily assured him that he had had a wonderful night's sleep. The manager looked distraught. 'A terrible thing has happened, Mr Rubinstein,' he said. 'The man in the room below yours. In the middle of the night . . . the chandelier fell on him!'

Last Passenger on Board is a Cissy

Years ago, when Iberia Airlines ran a contest to find a suitable advertising slogan, I submitted what I thought was the rather droll entry, 'Spanish Fly.' Needless to say, my name did not

30

figure among the list of winners. Knowing what I know now, I realise that countless members of the staff had probably thought of it already. On the whole, airline personnel adopt a robust, if not cynical, attitude to what is smugly regarded as 'the corporate image.'

Refuelling in Heathrow Airport's departure lounge one evening with a British Airways cabin crew, I was mildly shocked to hear them constantly referring to the respected flag-carrier as 'British Ashtrays'. My expression of surprise was greeted with a flood of equally inventive, and totally unjustified, distortions of other international airline names. Cathay Pathetic was the first, followed by Dan Dare, Swizzair, Un-Ibearable (or Dry-Beria, as a freeloading friend once called them when told they had forgotten to load the Champagne), El Ill, Aeroflop, Pain-American and, for the acronym TWA, 'Try Walking Across'.

Pausing only for you to cancel your flight tickets, all this may explain why you can never get any service when you press the call-button on long-distance flights. The cabin staff are all behind the curtain making up jokes. And when they finally do appear, they won't even let you into the fun-and-games. How strange that people who can be so hilarious off-duty can sometimes appear as sour as supermarket Soave when asked to perform the simplest service.

In a survey conducted on frequent business travellers, the magazine *Executive Travel* dredged up some splendid examples of non-service. A German stewardess told a British executive in grave need of a gin and tonic that the call button was 'for emergencies only': another forceful Fräulein insisted threateningly that German sparkling Riesling was 'genuine champagne' and a British Airways steward informed a teetotal company director that he could not have a glass of water as 'it is not available to Economy Class passengers.'

My personal Hostess-with-the-Leastest Award, however, must go to the gorgon with stainless-steel teeth who hid behind her curtain throughout the whole of a Bulgarian Airlines flight to Sofia. In desperation, and braving the consequences of that Medusa-like glance, I at last caught her eye and asked for a drink. 'No!' she replied, with implacable authority. 'It is only forty-five minutes to landing.'

Long-distance flights inevitably remind me of being in hospital. Every two hours somebody wakes you up and sticks orange juice in front of you. At any moment I expect them to say, 'And how are *we* this morning? Now pull your seat into the upright position and smarten yourself up because Doctor will be round in a few minutes . . . and we don't want you looking like *that*, do we?'

In the early days of package tours people dressed up in their Sunday best to fly abroad, and some airlines still cling to this reverential approach to travel. On a Press facility trip to the United States a few years ago, the public relations worrier in charge of the group thought he would do us all a good turn by upgrading us to First Class on the return flight. Unfortunately, the PR had left it to the last minute and the result was an exquisite Holiday Fiasco. The officer in charge at the check-in desk took one look at our slovenly attire and refused to let us on board. 'We have a dress code on this airline,' he sniffed. 'That means wearing a jacket and tie in the First Class section.' We desperately scoured our hand-baggage for jackets and ties and grumpily reappeared at the desk in some semblance of smartness. One writer's luggage had gone ahead, however, and all he had in his grip was the full evening dress he had worn at the previous night's gala dinner and dance.

The officer reluctantly sorted out our boarding cards, and then played a trump card of his own. 'There are six of you,' he said, 'but only five First Class seats are available. You will have to draw straws among yourselves for who gets left behind in Economy Class.' If you were on that particular flight and have always wondered why one passenger flew the whole way in Economy, sitting stiff and uncomfortable in black tie and dinner jacket, now you know the reason.

At least the poor chap got to his destination. Mr and Mrs William Colgan, who boarded an economy flight from Los

Angeles to Frankfurt, got no further than Baltimore. When the plane stopped to refuel, the couple, who were wearing matching grey jogging suits, were asked to leave. Apparently, they had transgressed the airline's dress regulations, which stipulated that economy passengers 'should be correctly attired in suits or sports jackets for men, dresses, skirts or trouser suits for women.' Finding themselves faced with an unexpected holiday stopover on the East Coast, Mr and Mrs Colgan asked for their luggage to be offloaded with the same speed and efficiency with which they had been 'shown the door.' Impossible, said the airline. Left on the Baltimore tarmac in the jogging suits they stood up in, Mr and Mrs Colgan watched their clothes, cosmetics and toiletries fly off to Germany. Peeved by all this, the couple sued the airline and were awarded $1,000 damages, just about enough to fly Economy to London and buy some new clothes at Marks & Spencer.

Considering the humiliation and inconvenience of it all, Mr and Mrs Colgan behaved with admirable restraint. On a Spanish plane there would have been a riot . . . unless the Royal Philharmonic Orchestra had been aboard to calm everyone down. In February 1986, a solo performance from the orchestra averted Latin mayhem when an Iberia airline Boeing 727 was delayed for three hours at Madrid airport on a flight to Valencia. The Spanish passengers created such a scene that the captain summoned the Guardia Civil. As three tough-looking guards armed with machine-guns boarded the plane, the orchestra's principal trumpet-player, Raymond Simmons, decided to defuse the situation with a virtuoso variation of the British stiff upper-lip. He took out his instrument and began to play *Viva Espana*. The other 103 members of the orchestra, who had watched the crowd grow restive, cheered. Waiting travellers, puzzled at first, applauded. The appropriate *paso doble*, *Valencia*, followed and by the time Mr Simmons had reached *Lady of Spain*, frayed Latin tempers had been soothed, though the passengers later filed seven foolscap sheets of complaint against the airline.

At the risk of sounding like Bleriot – or even Biggles – things were a sight more easy-going in the early days of air travel, when Imperial Airways flew with mahogany-panelled cabins (complete with bell-pulls for the servants), Heathrow was a collection of Nissen huts and the 'air hostesses' all came from Roedean College and had cut-glass accents which would have fractured a Waterford rose-bowl at twenty paces.

Old British European Airways hands still tell of the legendary pilot who would emerge from the cabin halfway through the flight, unwinding a ball of string. Handing one end to an appalled passenger, he would say, 'I'm just popping to the toilet. If you notice the plane veering to the left, pull the string once. If it moves to the right, tug the string twice.' And off he would walk towards the VACANT sign, whistling nonchalantly, while the passenger sat there petrified, his knuckles slowly whitening on the taut length of twine. They don't make 'em like that any more, which is probably a good thing.

Another pilot's favourite wheeze was to join the passengers as they entered the aircraft, dressed in a sports jacket and flannel trousers. Grabbing a spare seat, he would sit there impatiently until the time arrived for take-off. 'Bloody pilot isn't even here yet!' he would roar, with more than a hint of slurred speech. 'Not good enough. Bloody poor show!' Then,

lurching to his feet and brushing aside the restraining hands of the alarmed passengers, he would shout, 'I used to be in the RAF. Dozen bombing raids over Berlin! I can take this kite up. Just you watch.' To everyone's consternation, the flight-cabin door would slam behind him and the next thing was the revving of the engines, followed by a slight jolt as the plane taxied towards the runway and started accelerating. They say the drinks trolley did a roaring trade in double brandies in the first half hour after take-off.

My colleague Robin Dewhurst, travel editor of the *Sunday People*, had an equally nerve-racking experience in Gibraltar, without even leaving the ground. It was the night before he was due to fly off. Sitting in a bar in one of the less entrancing parts of town, he became fascinated by the repeated attempts of a burly, florid gentleman – as legless as an adder pickled in absinthe – to continue drinking, despite all the efforts of the barman to dissuade him. Throwing him out proved ineffective. Every time his seat was ejected, he would totter back, belligerently demanding 'Jusht one more for the road.' Robin left him at one in the morning, still demanding service in a voice which by now sounded like a loud-hailer choked with gravel. Imagine Robin's sinking heart at seven the same morning, seated in the plane, to see the pilot plodding heavily across the tarmac towards him. Yes, the same man from the bar.

It was not Robin's month for flying. A couple of weeks later, he was on a plane which seemed to be taking an interminable time in landing. Eventually, the pilot appeared with a screwdriver in his hand and lifted up a section of the carpeting in the gangway. Poking about with his screwdriver, the pilot was plainly relieved to hear a sudden click, followed by the sound of the undercarriage descending. A relief shared, in no small measure, by the passengers.

Another colleague of mine, a famous travel-writer, passed into aviation history with his dreadful reply to a well-meaning German Tourist Board official who asked him, 'Have you ever been to Cologne?' 'The last time I saw Cologne,' boomed my friend, 'was through a bomb-sight at five thousand feet!'

Luckily, there is justice in this world. The selfsame man was rendered speechless on a flight from Paris to London when a prankster in pilot's uniform appeared from the flight-deck wearing dark glasses, walking unsurely and gesturing ahead of him with a white stick.

Those were innocent days.

In-flight horror stories now seem to have taken over from the harmless fun and games. In another survey, a travel magazine asked its readers to submit their most quease-making airline experiences. The tally of classical frighteners included six hijacks, 53 cases of in-flight engine blowouts and/or locked landing gear, three crash landings, 11 lightning strikes, 23 bomb scares, 13 reports of food poisoning, 11 near misses (including evasive action to a flock of Indian vultures and a European dog on a runway) and two collisions with airport trucks.

After a seven-hour delay at Guangzhou Airport in China, one reader was finally informed that the aircraft was 'sick' and that a new one would be found. Two hours later, he was told, 'New aircraft more sick than first one, so will take first one.' Another traveller found himself queueing to board an internal Nigerian flight with what appeared to be the entire population of Lagos. It turned out the plane had been overbooked three times. The local military solved the problem in an ingenious way; they made all the passengers with boarding cards run round the plane twice and the winners of the race got the seats.

Passengers on a flight leaving Bangladesh for London were mystified by a persistent and increasingly hysterical hammering on the side of the plane as it stood on the tarmac. The cabin crew eventually opened the door . . . to reveal the pilot standing outside. The game of Spot the Pilot worked in reverse when an Icelandair domestic flight took off from Reykjavik, leaving the entire cabin crew drinking coffee in the airport lounge. The aircraft returned ten minutes later, after a tetchy passenger had knocked on the flight-deck door demanding to know where the stewardesses were. The crew were discovered still sitting in the lounge, unaware that they should have been 30,000 feet overhead.

One frequent flyer had his confidence dented when cabin

staff asked him to sit in the lavatory during take-off, so they could occupy the seats nearest the emergency exit. Another found himself recruited to hold the aircraft door closed at take-off and during landing, and on a Delta Airlines flight, a businessman was shown to a seat next to a man whose wicker lunch-basket contained a rattlesnake which he fed twice between Dallas and Atlanta.

Human fellow-passengers, however, can prove just as disconcerting. Imagine the twinge of unease which must have flickered across the face of Mr E. M. Wiltshire of Reading, Berkshire when a woman in tweedy suit and pearls turned to him on the flight from New York and asked haughtily, 'Where are we going?' Sensing trouble, Mr Wiltshire answered clearly and carefully, 'Heathrow.' 'I want to go to Bromley, Kent', said the woman impatiently, 'does it go there?' Before he could reply, she added with more than a hint of suspicion, 'How many stations do we stop at?'

Despite Mr Wiltshire's calming reassurance that it was a direct flight, the woman viewed the shuttered windows with some disdain and sniffed, 'How can I see which platform we are at? I hope I don't miss Bromley.' Diplomatically, Mr Wiltshire turned round and feigned sleep. When he awoke, the woman had gone. It was just like Alfred Hitchcock's film,

The Lady Vanishes. Had Mr Wiltshire imagined it all? Had the tweedy lady stepped out halfway across the Atlantic, assuming it was Bromley? Had she been trying to tell him something in code . . . and been silenced by enemy agents? Understandably, Mr Wiltshire didn't stop to find out. He was also first out of the Customs gate.

As the Irish comedian, Dave Allen, once remarked, 'Wonderful thing, jet travel. How else can you have breakfast in London, lunch over Rome and dinner in New York, while your luggage goes on to Yokohama?' As one who is drawn to Lost Luggage counters like an alcoholic to a cocktail bar, I can sympathise with those solitary figures who stand at airport carousels, long after the rest of the passengers have gone, staring hopefully at the baggage-opening, but knowing deep down that their cases will never appear.

The mere memory of a Press trip with the late Lord Thomson – who at that time owned *The Times*, the *Sunday Times*, Thomson Holidays *and* an airline – fills me with a warm and reassuring glow. There were about 150 of us on the plane, bound for some freeloading jamboree in Majorca. All our luggage was crammed into the hold, except for one suitcase, that belonging to Lord Thomson himself.

We had watched, suitably impressed, as Lord Thomson's valise had been personally conveyed by a lackey to some remote and secure part of the aircraft, far from the vulgar imitation-leather, glossy PVC and common canvas of the herd. At Palma, the only suitcase which failed to appear was Lord Thomson's. Somehow, it had vanished on the way. 'The Spanish police', commented one unsympathetic wag, 'are probably treating it as an open-and-shut case.'

It could have been worse. A businessman travelling from Stockholm to Gothenberg had his suitcase mis-labelled and put aboard the wrong aircraft. A spot security check of luggage on the other flight revealed no apparent owner for the bag. So Swedish anti-terrorist militia blew it up from a safe distance, toothbrush, souvenirs and all.

Maybe it is not surprising that airline staff tend to keep

their jokes to themselves these days – though, for unconscious humour, I love the riposte delivered by a girl at
Manchester Airport's information desk when an unsuspecting American tourist asked, 'Where's the mail-drop?' In
the frostiest tone of voice, and no doubt pondering on the
crudity of American slang, the girl replied, 'Gent's toilet, first
on the left, sir.'

Common Touch

It pays to enunciate your destination clearly when hailing a
taxi, or you might end up on an expensive variation of the
magical mystery tour. In London for a rapid business-cum-
cultural stopover, the late Sam Spiegel, the producer of movie
blockbusters like *Bridge on the River Kwai*, leapt into a cab
outside his hotel with the intention of spending an improving
hour at the Tutankhamun exhibition, then drawing huge
crowds. 'Tutankhamun!' he snapped briskly to the driver, in
his rich Viennese accent. A suspiciously long while later, the
taxi rolled to a halt in what appeared to be a deserted waste-
land, far from any sign of civilisation, Egyptian or otherwise.
'Here you are', said the driver, 'Tooting Common.'

Culture Shock

When it is absolutely imperative that diplomatic relations
should be as smooth and tactful as possible, you can be sure
that someone will put his foot in it. It is not often, however,
that the culprit is a poodle. A delegation of United States
senators and economic pundits travelled to Iran to meet the
Shah, at a particularly fragile point in relations between the

40

two countries. Among the party was the cultural expert, Mrs Albert Brockman, together with her black poodle, Gigolo, to which she was devoted. The plane arrived in Teheran eleven hours late, but a full guard of honour was still assembled, with the Shah himself standing stiffly to attention at the foot of the steps. The first one off the plane was not the leading senator, but Gigolo, bursting for a pee and anxious to find anything that resembled a tree. The nearest thing was the Shah. Unable to move, the King of Kings had to watch helplessly as Gigolo cocked his leg and amply watered his uniform trousers and sparkling shoes. This was not the last that was seen of Gigolo. At a formal reception and banquet the next day Mrs Brockman was late. Arriving alone by cab, and inevitably clutching Gigolo, she dashed up the staircase of the Shah's palace and flung open the immense double doors at the top. It was the wrong staircase. But the assembled dignitaries, in a textbook example of conditioned response, immediately turned towards her, assuming it was the Shah. When the real Shah arrived seconds later at the other entrance to the room, it was to find his entire court and guests with their backs to him, bowing, curtseying and in some cases prostrating themselves for the benefit of Mrs Brockman and her dog.

All in the Past

John Herdman, the gregarious general manager of the Imperial Hotel in Blackpool, pulled his first pint of beer in 1936. Every year he holds a party in the bar to celebrate, with all the drinks at pre-war prices . . . 3p for a pint of bitter, 15p for a whisky. On John's fiftieth anniversary, in 1986, an hotel guest drifted into the party unawares and was surprised to be charged only a few pence for his glass of scotch. He had several more at the same price before slipping out to the telephone and ringing a couple of friends forty miles away. 'Get down to the Imperial right now,' he told them. 'They're giving the booze away!' An hour later the thirsty pair arrived by car. But by now the party had broken up and the bar prices had reverted to normal. Three double scotches cost them £8, plus the price of their petrol.

Welcome Home 1

One of the joys of travel is the opportunity it presents to meet people from other countries and compare the differences in one's way of life. That is the theory, anyway. It all went wrong when Mrs Josephine Williams of Coventry went with her two sisters to Heathrow Airport to meet a long-lost brother. She succeeded in 'kidnapping' a total stranger.

The victim was an innocent American tourist who had just tottered off the plane in a duty-free haze. Before the poor man could say 'Howdy', he had been smothered in kisses by Mrs Williams and her sisters and ushered into a parked car. By the time he realised what was happening, he was well on his way up the M1 motorway.

The women first suspected all was not well when the man, now sober and terrified, tried to jump out of the moving car. When they told him he was being taken to a family reunion, he pleaded, 'Here's my wallet. Take my money and let me go'. The women were on the outskirts of Coventry before the American eventually persuaded them they had got the wrong man. 'I thought from the beginning he wasn't my brother,' Mrs Williams said later, 'but my sisters wouldn't listen. They said I was only twelve when he left for America and I wouldn't remember.'

Welcome Home 2

Most British holiday resorts pall after a time and well within a fortnight you start looking around for day-trips, preferably to somewhere new and exciting. So Mr William Farmer and his wife, Nora, jumped at the chance of joining a British Rail 'magical mystery tour' from their resort at Newport, Monmouthshire. The whole point of the BR tours is not to let the customers know where they are going – it is all part of the fun – but on the eight-hour round trip Mr and Mrs Farmer's train only stopped once, at Margate, in Kent. An attractive spot, except for one thing. Mr and Mrs Farmer had travelled magically and mysteriously right back to their home town. While the other passengers raced off to explore, Mr and Mrs Farmer passed the time by returning to their own house to open the mail, have lunch . . . and look forward to getting back on holiday.

Tourist Traps and Terrible Souvenirs

Clutching his guitar, the calypso singer leaped out from behind the bushes where he had been lurking in wait for the tourist coach. As the visitors piled out, he realised he had netted the biggest catch since Captain Ahab wiped the salt spray from his telescope and cried, 'Thar she blows!' A coach-load of VIPs, no less.

The visitors, who had been touring Trinidad on an airline promotional campaign, smiled indulgently as King Calypso launched into a series of apparently spontaneous verses in their honour. Flattering was hardly the word. The men in the group were compared to the great heroes of history and legend, Alexander the Great, Lord Byron, Caesar, Terry Wogan. The beauty of the women, crooned King Calypso, would make Bo Derek look like Mr Hyde when the anti-toxin ran out.

Being VIPs, the visitors adopted that expression of simulated demur which indicated they heartily agreed with every word. Among the more worldly VIPs, however, suspicions were beginning to crystallise even before King Calypso launched into a final verse which struck an all-too-familiar chord, 'T'ank you greatly for lis'nin to me, now I know you'll treat me most gen'rously.' The guitar vanished, to be replaced by an empty hat. It was a Tourist Trap.

The calypso singers of Trinidad, not content with highway robbery at the point of a guitar, have added an extra refinement of their own. If you do not 'tip gen'rously,' you are likely to be serenaded with verses of a less complimentary nature, to put it mildly. The freeloading VIPs, King Calypso discovered to his dismay, all suffered from an unfortunate disability: short arms and long pockets. With the handouts failing to come up to expectations, the tone of the calypsos changed abruptly. After a brisk succession of libellous verses, King Calypso struck a curdling chord and fired his parting shot, 'Who are these tourists who are so mean? They're the tightest trippers we've ever seen.'

Every country has its tourist traps and it has been my misfortune to stumble into a wide variety of them. The stubs of my travellers' cheques prove conclusively the theory that some people are born victims, their fate predetermined by congenital flaws in their character.

I have been lured into 'liqueur tastings' in Majorcan hooch factories, thinly disguised as typical *bodegas*, where each concoction tasted more nauseating than the one before. After the tenth glass I would have signed anything, which is probably why HM Customs occasionally remind me that they still hold ten gallons of some frightful green liquid in bond on my behalf. In Moroccan carpet-weaving sheds, I've sipped mint tea by the bucketful, trying vainly to put off the moment when the vast, bilious-looking rug I had been forced into admiring was finally wrapped up and thrust across my shoulders for the incredibly low price of £400, 'Because the Eengleesh are our oldest friends, *Effendi.*'

Times beyond number, I have been steered by so-called guides into 'traditional handicrafts exhibitions' which turned out to be souvenir shops staffed mainly by reformed pickpockets whose idea of repaying their debt to society is to press hundreds of rubbishy wallets on anyone luckless enough to cross their path. After one bulk purchase, I thought all my Christmas present problems had been solved for ever, but the ingratitude of one's friends knows no bounds. Since the wallets operate on a mysterious 'self-destruct' system, and fall apart under the pressure of a Barclaycard and a 50p book of stamps, one would have thought that friends would have been only too delighted to receive a new one each Yuletide.

The fact that my home boasts more brass ashtrays than the entire allocation for the NAAFI in World War Two is the result of an encounter with the persuasive owner of a 'Traditional Toledo-ware factory' whose staff of apprentices started hammering away like the dwarfs in Niebelheim the instant I appeared under the sign saying 'Please look around – No obligation to buy.'

At least I ended up with something to show (often in large quantities) for these skirmishes. On the completely negative side, there are tourist traps where you are lucky to emerge with the clothes you stand up in.

I have flogged up the banks of the Rhine, following a series of signposts pointing to 'The Famous View', to discover that it was only obtainable from the restricted vantage-point of a cafe terrace where £5, it was explained, allowed me to feast my eyes on the panorama while sipping a cup of acorn coffee. In Tangier I was left stranded in the middle of the Kasbah after paying a guide £4 to lead me there, on the naïve assumption that it also entitled me to be led out again. And in Granada my last 500–peseta note was plucked from my hand in a pair of castanets, wielded expertly by one of those gypsy cave-dwellers on the Sacromonte who break into frenzied 'impromptu flamenco fiestas' with their aunts, cousins and offspring at the sight of any tourist with two coins to rattle together.

The further afield you venture, the more cunningly laid is the ambush. For inspired greed, few Tourist Trappers can rival the priests of Lalibela, in Ethiopia, who until recently ruled their domain with an iron rod of rapacity. Lalibela's network of underground churches, hewn out of the living rock 600 years ago, is one of the undisputed wonders of the world, equalled only by the clergy's system of extorting money from visitors. There is, or was, a set fee of around £3 to enter the churches (the priests had their 'spies' in Lalibela's only hotel to make sure no tourist got through the net), but that is merely the introductory offer. Inside each chapel, priests carrying illuminated Bibles and silver crosses pose obligingly in their colourful vestments. Just as all the visitors are getting their Nikons in a twist, the priests step aside to reveal strategically placed wooden bowls overflowing with dollar bills.

It is not a simple matter of discreetly dropping something into the offertory box. The sanctity of the church, it is hinted, is disturbed less by the rustle of folding money than the vulgar jangle of base coin. In case you still have not got the message, the priests fix the photographers with a steady gaze and gesture pointedly at the bowls. Touring all ten churches can prove a more arduous penance than shuffling three times round St Peter's Square on your knees. 'Maybe', suggested one visitor, whose milk of human kindness could have been marketed by the churnful, 'Maybe the whole thing has been devised as a test of one's faith.' Reports filtering back from Ethiopia indicate that the left-wing government may have curbed the worst excesses of the Lalibela clergy; but considering their powers of survival, I doubt it.

A latter-day Aladdin, who used to flit among the ruins of

Carthage, in Tunisia, selling 'genuine Roman oil lamps' to tourists, almost qualified for the Duke of Edinburgh's Award for Industry. Like an Arabian Nights genie, he would pop up from behind a column and whisper, 'Psst! I work here and I found these little pottery lamps while digging around. I'm supposed to hand in everything I find, but I can let you have one for two dirhams.' With its none-too-subtle hint that the stuff had fallen off the back of a chariot, coupled with the opportunity of snaffling a relic from under the noses of the museum authorities, the offer was irresistible. Hundreds of tourists had furtively slipped the little lamps into their pockets before one sharp-eyed Briton spotted the salesman collecting fresh stock from a shop in town, which displayed in its window the notice, 'Reproduction Roman oil lamps, one dirham.'

Sharp eyes, and a few preliminary enquiries, might have prevented the hideous embarrassment experienced by a British business-traveller in Hong Kong, who decided to buy an unusual 'ethnic' gift for his wife. He found exactly what he was looking for in a rather sinister little antique shop behind Hollywood Road; one of those inky dens, stuffed with lacquer and porcelain, which look like the setting for a Fu Manchu thriller. It was a bronze medallion, slightly bigger than a 50p piece, embossed with exotic-looking Chinese characters, bearing an official-looking seal on the back and suspended from a chain. 'Eighteenth Centuly' warbled the shopkeeper, 'velly rare.'

Back in England, the man's wife was delighted with the present and made up her mind to wear it at a reception given by her husband's board of directors for a Chinese trade delegation. The instant she appeared at the reception, the medallion swinging like a pendulum, all conversation stopped and the Chinese guests froze in mid-gesture, their faces registering varying shades of affront and dismay. One of the delegates hissed something to the managing director, who leaped forward as if electrified by a cattle prod and hustled the wife into the corridor. 'That medallion,' he squealed, 'take it off! Do you know what it says?' Glancing warily to each side, the MD repeated through clenched teeth the translation his guest had supplied, 'Registered Prostitute Number 95. Licensed and certified free of disease by Kowloon Department of Health and Hygeine.'

Souvenirs frequently have the reverse effect to that intended; they can be depressing things. It is a painful sight to stand at any big airport and watch the holidaymakers returning, loaded down with leaky Spanish wineskins, cracked castanets, beer mugs that play 'The Chicken Song,' moulting camel saddles, Eiffel Tower doorstops, Leaning Tower of Pisa paperweights and models of the Last Supper made from seashells and bits of broken mirror. All of it doomed to the dustbin. Hideous to start with, most souvenirs look a thousand times worse when you get them home, where they lurk reproachfully in the lounge or glare balefully at you from the mantelpiece. Paradoxically, souvenirs do not travel.

Even the most sophisticated globe-trotters succumb to the souvenir temptation. The actor, Robert Morley, has admitted publicly, 'One particularly crowded parking lot in my sitting room includes a Delft china windmill, a silver spinning wheel, a cuckoo emerging from an ivory egg, a folding mirror from Palma, cocktail swords from Toledo, a swear box from Torquay and the Eiffel Tower masquerading as a thermometer.'

The columist, Keith Waterhouse, tells how he entered the 'Nothing to Declare' channel at Heathrow airport, carrying a souvenir from Capri in the shape of a flower-market stall made of twisted wire, and housing a miniature cactus in a pot. He was stopped by a Customs officer, who informed him that attempting to import a 'living thing' was a punishable offence. Waterhouse was eventually allowed to keep the Living Thing after signing a declaration that he would not part with it for at least a year (even though it should become a Dead Thing in the meanwhile) and that he would hold it in readiness for examination by the Ministry of Agriculture's inspector 'at any reasonable hour'. Some souvenir.

The greatest souvenir-collectors of all time, of course, were the British aristocracy. No model flower-stalls from Capri for them. They collected on an epic scale. Lord Elgin carried off a respectable part of the frieze from the Parthenon – the Greeks still keep asking for it back – and in Castle Howard you can see a large section of the Delphic Altar, carted away by a previous lord of the manor. 'Souvenir hunting' on that scale should make you feel a lot better the next time you stuff a hotel towel into your suitcase.

The patron saint of the souvenir trade must surely be the medieval king who, when his son vanished from home, vowed, 'If he is alive and well, I will present a statue to the city showing him exactly as he was found.' It seemed a good idea at the time but, as luck would have it, the moment the searchers stumbled across him, the lost boy was relieving himself. As good as his word, the king commissioned a statue of his son in the form of a fountain, and so gave birth to millions of the most excruciating souvenirs ever inflicted on a long-suffering public. The statue is the famous Manneken-

Pis, whose merry jet of water still tinkles away in the centre of Brussels. You can buy the Manneken-Pis in every shape and form; there are Manneken bars of soap, Manneken corkscrews, Manneken table mats, even Manneken spirit-pourers, with your best Glenfiddich coming out of you-know-where. One of the most successful lines is a life-size model in plaster with internal plumbing, which acts as a garden fountain.

On a coach tour through Italy, I was once led through the dank and aromatic back streets of Venice to what purported to be a Venetian glass-works. The rest of the passengers watched spellbound as the glassblowers churned out kitschy glass animals by the thousand, wine glasses so twisted you would not have known where to put your lip and sets of fruit bowls writhing, Laocoon-like, with blue and green stripes. All over the world, the words 'showroom,' 'factory' or 'outlet' are euphemisms for 'souvenir shop,' and the show-

room to which we were shunted afterwards was a chamber of horrors of garish and grotesque glassware. Back on the coach, as we sped mercifully away, I piped up loudly, 'I bet nobody bought any of that dreadful rubbish.' There was an uncomfortable silence, broken only by a delicate but persistent chinking from the overhead luggage racks. They were crammed with cardboard boxes, all full of Venetian glass. It was a textbook example of H. L. Mencken's dictum, 'Nobody ever lost a fortune underestimating the public taste'; and nobody on the coach trip spoke to me again.

These days no country is so remote, inaccessible or poverty-stricken that it does not boast a clutch of souvenir shops in some strategic tourist position. In emergent, or even submergent, countries the prime location for snaring travellers is the airport departure lounge. It is a cunning move, particularly in countries whose currencies are so insubstantial that no British bank clerk would even be bothered to clean his spectacles with the banknotes.

Since you cannot change your money back into sterling, you are left swapping your leftover lek, kwanza, ngultrums, pulas, birr, bututus, cory, kip, at, avos, tambala, khoums, won, jun, chon, mongo, dong, ngwee or stotinki for some dreadful artefact stamped, 'souvenir of Gagaland.' The late James Cameron, author and inveterate traveller, reckoned

that all souvenir shops in airports were run by relatives of
the local currency control staff. After the visitors had disappeared, clutching their grisly mementoes, the proceeds were
shared out.

The strange thing about souvenirs is that they transcend
all national barriers. Wherever you go, from Skegness to the
Niagara Falls, from Benidorm to the banks of the Orinoco,
they are all the same. The whole world is stuffed from cellar
to attic with identical leather wallets, copper hunting horns,
glass animals, snowfall paperweights, curved Arab daggers
and recycled vests which say, 'My folks went to the Sey-
chelles but all I got was this rotten tee-shirt'. It is, one can
only conclude, some sort of international conspiracy to
subvert public taste; terrorism by trash.

Some countries still try to preserve their national identity
with hideous specialities of their own. I once recoiled in
genuine horror from a coffee-table, on sale in Nairobi,
supported gracefully but sickeningly on three real zebra-legs.
A friend possesses a miniature electric-chair labelled
'souvenir of Alcatraz' and in Las Vegas you can buy a pair

52

of men's underpants showing a pair of dice and the words, 'I shot crap in Las Vegas.'

It is almost a relief to turn to Spain, where the armchair *torero* can order a mock bullfight poster with his name printed among the genuine performers. The result is often less than *macho*. A 'sample' on show in the Calle San Miguel, in Torremolinos, trumpets *'Magnifica Corrida de Toros!,'* followed by the resounding roll-call, 'Featuring El Cordobes, Luis Dominguin, Antonio Ordonez and Sid'. Not even El Sid, at that.

Souvenirs are big business. Just before the wedding of Prince Charles and Lady Diana Spencer, souvenir companies insured themselves for £15 million against postponement of the happy event; a calamity which would have left them with egg on their faces and millions of useless gewgaws on their shelves. This fate actually overtook over-optimistic manufacturers during the Pope's visit to Britain in 1982. Hundreds of tons of unsold memorabilia, from papal teaspoons to carriage clocks, were still languishing in warehouses a year later; including two tons of diaries, printed in Eire, which started the year in April. 'It is God's justice, if you like,' said one philosophical marketing manager. 'Traders made a killing during Prince Charles's wedding and expected a similar bonanza.' Is God against souvenirs? It is a tempting thought.

With the amount of money involved, maybe we should take the subject a great deal more seriously. But do not repeat the mistake made by a distinguished colleague on his first visit to Russia, that Ireland of the East where nothing is ever what it seems.

Before he left, do-gooding friends suggested he took as many English newspapers and paperbacks as he could, since young people in Russia could not get their hands on them and, anyway, they were useful for making friends or swapping for the odd ikon. When he stepped off the Polish cruise-liner *Stefan Batory* in Leningrad harbour, he must have looked like a cross between W. H. Smith's and Foyle's Bargain Basement. Before you could say *Morning Star*, he was surrounded by crowds of young students begging for books, magazines, newspapers . . . anything that would give them an uncensored glimpse of life in western Europe. Smugly, and no doubt feeling like an early pioneer of the SPCK, he handed over all the reading-matter he had brought with him. After profuse thanks and assurances of everlasting Anglo-Soviet friendship, the youngsters vanished into the night. His missionary work was done. A week later, while polishing off a bottle of Polish vodka with the captain of the *Batory*, he realised he had been hoodwinked with a vengeance. The students, explained the captain, had all been young Communist 'trusties', whose job was to waylay unsuspecting Western visitors, persuade them to hand over any subversive literature they had brought . . . and then burn the lot.

Wine Some, Lose Some

You may have snivelled during *Gone With the Wind*, blubbed during *Love Story* and broken down halfway through *E.T.*, but be prepared to weep buckets for Rupert Denny, former Wine Correspondent of the *Daily Telegraph*, who booked in at a remote hotel in Oughterard, County Galway, for an Irish fishing holiday.

On his first night, he took his seat in the small and deserted dining-room and was immediately served a pot of tea by a senile waiter dressed in a crumpled dinner-jacket seemingly covered with lichen. 'Haven't you got any wine?' enquired Rupert, already prepared to settle for a carafe of the most ill-natured plonk. 'Sure, nobody ever asks for wine here,' replied the waiter. Then he paused. 'Wait a minute, I think there may be a few bottles of the stuff left in the cellar.'

After what seemed an eternity, the waiter reappeared brushing the cobwebs from an old, hand-written wine list which had manifestly not seen the light of day for a decade. It was now 1954 and the list had probably been gathering dust since before World War Two. Rupert was about to forget the whole idea when he caught sight of the names on the list. He could not believe his eyes. Not only were they the noblest vintages but the prices, in old British shillings and pence, were absurdly low. Chateau Latour Haut Brion 1931, 12s 6d, Echezaux 1938, 11s 6d, Chassagne-Montrachet 1934, 15s.

The waiter had been right. They hadn't sold a bottle in years, and they were still at pre-war prices! Barely concealing the tremble in his voice, and fearing that it might all be a dream, Rupert ordered a Hospice de Beaune 1935 at 14s 6d. The wait was agonising, but the waiter finally tottered back with a dusty bottle in his hands and Rupert forced himself to look at the label. It could not be true, but it was. It was the priceless wine he had ordered, no doubt about it. 'Is this right then, sor?' asked the waiter. 'It certainly is,' sighed Rupert, mentally savouring the nectar in anticipation. 'Then I'll just give it a good shake up, sor, as all the goodness has gone to the bottom.' And with that, the waiter up-ended the bottle and started shaking it vigorously. They do say that, from that moment on, Rupert was never known to smile again.

Train of Coincidence

In the months just before World War Two, thousands of Jews grasped their last chance to flee from Nazi Germany and occupied Austria before the frontier gates closed down on them for ever. Some risked carefully planned, but risky, illegal escape routes. Others took the chance of being stripped of all their possessions and deported. Many failed to get through at all. One of the luckiest was Oscar Straus, composer of popular operettas like *The Chocolate Soldier*. He decided to bluff his way through by merely buying a railway ticket in Vienna and crossing the frontier by train, hoping not to be recognised; a plan which his friends regarded as suicidal. But Straus was determined. In the railway compartment, however, a man in civilian clothes who had been eyeing him suspiciously for some time, suddenly blurted out, 'You are Oscar Straus, and I take it you are trying to flee the country.' Straus went rigid with terror. But the man's next words were completely unexpected. 'My parents fell in love after seeing one of your operettas, so one could say that, but for you, I should not be here. I am the Gauleiter of the frontier district and I will see you encounter no difficulties.' The man was as good as his word. Straus left Austria safely, to find eventual haven in the United States.

Key Witness

Never lend your car keys to a friend. It might end up less than a good turn. Ingrid Christopherson, former manager of the British Women's Ski Team, lent the keys of her Toyota Cressida to a colleague in Wengen, Switzerland. The car, though covered in snow and standing in a crowded car-park, was easily identifiable; it was grey and had a roof rack. The friend got into the driving seat, switched on and happily accelerated off in the direction of Austria . . . leaving Ingrid's Toyota still standing there. The friend had driven off the wrong car, a 'double' which, by pure coincidence, had been parked only a few spaces away. Although the mistake was soon discovered, it took three weeks to recover the Toyota's *doppelganger* from Austria. 'In the meantime,' said Ingrid, 'the Swiss police treated me like a criminal.' As if all this was not enough, the owner of the other car demanded 657 Swiss francs (around £230) compensation; unimpressed by a Toyota spokeman's claim that 'the chances of two identical-model cars parked near to one another and with identical keys must be many millions to one'.

Farewell Appearance

Art is an illusion, and nowhere is this more true than at the Alcazar, the Parisian cabaret-nightclub near St-Germain-des-Prés, which has been packing in the tourists for twenty years. In all that time, nothing has ever succeeded in ruffling the urbanity of the patron, Jean-Marie Rivière. One night, a British visitor went to the men's toilet and died there of an overdose of drugs. The staff found the corpse but could not think how to get rid of it discreetly, seeing that the only exit from the toilet led right across the club. Undaunted, Rivière draped the body in a huge *tricolor* and, to the strains of Chopin's Funeral March, had four waiters bear it out aloft through the midst of the diners, who roared applause at what they thought the best item in the show. It is no coincidence that the phrase *sang-froid* is French.

I'm Sorry, Sir, but the Wine Waiter is Corked

The British tourist had read all about wine and, unlike the plebs at the next table, knew exactly what to do when the waiter carefully poured the first few drops in his glass. Casually sniffing the bouquet, he swirled the glass gently, took a delicate sip and rolled the velvety liquid to the back of his throat. You could have heard his cry the other side of Venice. 'My God!' he shrieked, 'What *is* this?'

The food squad of the Italian police asked the same question when they raided the winery where the rotgut had come from and found hundreds of barrels bearing eminently

respectable names like Chianti and Frascati. Later forty-two people were arrested on charges of producing ersatz wine for the tourist trade. The ingredients included figs, oxblood, chemicals, dates, beans and dried apple, with a little unprocessed grape juice to give the stuff the right flavour.

It was a product in the worst possible taste and, mercifully, this incident occurred a long time before the tragic Italian wine scandal of 1986, when many people died from drinking wine adulterated with poisonous methyl alcohol.

My hero used to be Toulouse Lautrec; not specifically for his painting, but for his attitude towards water. At dinner parties, he made a theatrical gesture of putting goldfish in the water carafe, explaining to a succession of startled guests that 'Water is only fit for fishes'. The comedian, W. C. Fields, put it even more bluntly. 'Never drink water,' he warned. 'Fishes make love in it.'

Nowadays I'm not so sure. After exposure for many years to some of the vilest vintages ever trodden by human foot, or concocted in a laboratory retort, I am inclined to agree with the Chinese sage who said, 'With the first glass, man drinks wine. With the second glass, wine drinks wine. Third glass, wine drinks man.'

Unlike the British tippler who so narrowly escaped Death in Venice, you do not have to go as far as to drink the stuff to risk getting a terminal hangover. There are some wines whose mere label is enough to make the hardest boozer blench. In a restaurant in Rouen, I was once served with a bottle proudly labelled *Chateau de Tremble*. It sounded more like a home for elderly alcoholics than a vineyard. Believe it or not, I have actually drunk a Spanish wine called *El Bollox* and another labelled *El Baterio* (which certainly tasted as though it would have been better for my Exide than my inside). And whatever possessed one sherry firm to call their product *Coma*?

Well-travelled and strong-stomached readers of this book will also recognise the Spanish *Sanvin* and Jordanian *Latrun* wines, both with their unfortunate suggestion of something to do with sanitation. But what do you make of *Buzbag*? Is it the alcoholic equivalent of a doggy-bag, for carrying leftover drinks from parties? A slang term for the breathalyser? A rude word for a female toper? Not at all; merely a red wine from Turkey.

Quite the worst gunge that ever sucked the fillings from my teeth came from a wicker-covered flask labelled 'Chianti' which was sneaked on to my table during a meal at a game lodge in Tanzania. One sip was enough to have me clutching at my throat and snatching for the bottle at the same time. Sure enough the label said Chianti. But underneath, in letters more miniscule than the small print on a fly-by-night insurance policy, were the sobering words, 'Produce of Ethiopia.'

The shock to the system was the same as that experienced by the former Fleet Street columist, Rance Pochin-Johnson, who was offered a cut-price bottle of scotch while on holiday in Italy. Again, the first sip turned out to be the last. One look at the label confirmed his worst fears. It said, 'Genuine Shotch Wisky. As brewed in the House of Lords by King George VI. Produce of Palermo.'

With unaccustomed levity, the *Sunday Telegraph* once offered a prize (a magnum of Ethiopian Chianti, second prize two magnums of Ethiopian Chianti) for the most amusing name for an imaginary Australian wine. The writer threw in his own suggestion, Billablanc. Rejecting the Cabernet of Dr Caligari as too recondite, I submitted Kangarouge instead. The winner, however, was the veritably throat-shrivelling Bondi Bleach.

Why they all bothered, I don't know. The names of actual Australian wines are extraordinary enough for anyone, like the Barossa Valley dry red which labours under the name of Bullamankanka.

All this brings me, most reluctantly, to Mick's Rotten Red – not a drop sold till it is two hours old – a wine which has done for Australian viniculture what Sweeney Todd did for the pork pie industry. This outrageous brew is actually sold over the counter from grim, flagon-size bottles at The Harrow, an old-established oiling-place into which I was once frogmarched by some colleagues from the Street of Shame.

The label said it all. 'An unusual, rough-as-guts red wine that has the distinctive bouquet of old and ill-cared-for animals', it informs the connoisseur. 'It is best drunk with the teeth clenched to prevent the ingestion of seeds and skins.' Much of the label is unprintable, but it ends resoundingly, 'Avoid contact with the eyes and open cuts. Keep away from naked flames.' Is it a joke? A challenge to the most depraved Kalgoolie cane-cutter? Sheer Aussie bravado? According to the label, the producers of this infernal broth are Swanville Estates, Western Australia. If you are visiting friends and relations Down Under, beware of Unidentifiable Flagon-like Objects in the sideboard. You have been warned.

At least one Australian escaped from Mick's Rotten Red to the more rarefied realms of viniculture. Mr Arthur Hennessy, owner of a modest off-licence in a remote area of Australia, came into a windfall and decided to take a wine tour of Europe. To his delight, he was treated as an honoured guest wherever he went. Distinguished French wine producers showed him round their cellars, rare vintages were uncorked, splendid meals laid on. Mr Hennessy returned home, still wondering why he had received the full VIP treatment; not realising that everyone thought he had been a far-flung member of the Hennessy brandy family.

It is the immutable fate of humorists like myself to be overtaken by reality before the ink is dry; and that certainly goes for imaginary Australian wine names.

One of the odder repercussions of the great Austrian Wine Scandal was that some some countries got totally confused and thought the adulterated plonko came from Australia. The scare began when thousands of bottles of Austrian wine were found to contain diethylene-glycol, a substance which northern Europeans pour into car radiators as 'anti-freeze'. In Japan, the confusion between Austrian and Australian wines became so acute that the Prime Minister himself, Mr Yasuhiro Nakasone, actually suggested to an Aussie trade delegate that their wine should be renamed 'Canberra' or even 'Koala', after the bear. Now, would *you* drink a wine labelled 'Bear's White'? Bear's white *what?* you might rightly ask.

The Austrian Wine Scandal was still rumbling on a year later, as more tainted supplies were discovered. Personally, I suspect that you would have to drink 5,000 gallons of the stuff before it would have the slightest effect. On the other hand, if your blood is still boiling after walking five miles through three feet of snow, you know someone has been secretly feeding you with Austrian blanco.

One cannot help feeling sorry, though, for the Austrian Institute in London, who accidentlly stumbled on a foolproof method of keeping freeloaders and gatecrashers away from receptions. Their invitation to a private art show at the Mall Galleries ended with the words, 'Admit two. Austrian wine'. Unfortunately, hardly anyone else turned up either.

None of this would have worried Sir Winston Churchill, whose attitude to wine was predictably robust. During World War Two, when the mere mention of anything German was tantamount to treason, Sir Winston was caught in his club drinking a bottle of vintage hock. 'How can you possibly drink German wine at a time like this?' protested a stuffy fellow-member. 'I'm not drinking it,' boomed Sir Winston, 'I'm *interning* it!'

Sir Winston would no doubt have suggested internment for the wine waiter – spotted by a *Good Food Guide* inspector on patrol in Ipswich – who stopped at a table, showed a couple the wine they had selected, and then drew the cork with his teeth. This macho performance, the gastronomic equivalent of biting away the pins of hand grenades, was no doubt intended to intimidate the diners. Wine waiters have a long history of arrogance towards their guests, as anyone who has ever ordered the cheapest bottle on a wine list will confirm.

Their rudeness does not normally extend as far as that of a restaurant in New York, where a British tourist complained, quite reasonably, that the wine a waiter had recommended was too sweet. Jutting out his chin in an alarmingly aggressive manner, the waiter exploded, 'Whaddya want, then, Mac? *Sour* wine?' No, the truclence of the wine waiter takes subtler forms, particularly when the fellow elevates himself to the rank of *sommelier*, complete with his 'badge of office,' the little tasting-cup hanging from a chain round the neck.

At a pretentiously overblown restaurant in Orlando, Florida, famous for its tourist trade, a *sommelier* dressed like Henry VIII – with a *tastevin* as big as a spittoon – wasted twenty minutes of everyone's precious drinking time decanting a youthful burgundy into a cut-glass port decanter. The wine could not have coughed up a speck of sediment if you had wrung its neck, yet this character gravely carried out his routine in front of a lighted candle, as if he had dragged up some venerable, cobweb-encrusted vintage from the cellars of Versailles. For once, we turned down the offer of a second bottle. Life is too short.

Tempus fugit was obviously on the mind of Lord Stockton when, at a formal banquet, he noticed that the glasses had not been filled for half an hour. All attempts to catch an eye having failed, Lord Stockton rose majestically to his feet, tapped his empty glass and said, 'I would like to propose a toast to absent friends . . . coupled with that of the wine waiter.'

Lord Stockton's pursuit of the wayward wine bottle may also have been prompted by the recent discovery that wine produces its own natural chemicals, which act as a useful disinfectant. Yes, it is the news we have all been waiting for; wine is antiseptic and therefore good for you. Pass it on. A

team of Canadian researchers discovered that red wine added to unhealthy water can make it safer to drink by reducing the activity of a wide range of gastric viruses, and a strain of polio virus was reduced in strength one thousand times by incubating it in grape juice for twenty-four hours. If that isn't good enough reason for asking your GP to prescribe a dozen bottles of *Marques de Caceres Gran Reserva 1978*, then I don't know what is.

Maybe it is the medicinal qualities of the wine which impel huge crowds of tourists to visit the Spanish-champagne cellars in San Sadurni, near Barcelona. At the Codorniu cellar, visited by 300,000 people a year, a group of British tourists couldn't help noticing a couple of young men who tagged on to the end of their party. The pair couldn't get the free wine down fast enough, and as each tray of 'samples' came round, their arms flashed out with the speed of a chameleon's tongue. 'Pushing it a bit, aren't you?' said one of the Britons, in a slightly disapproving way, as their seventh glass of bubbly went down the hatch. To the man's astonishment, they chorussed, 'He that is without sin, let him cast the first stone,' adding for good measure, '*John 8, 7*'. It turned out they were both theological students, and Irish, what's more, on their day off from a local seminary.

The most stupendous collection of booze in the world is, indeed, in Spain, though not a drop of it will ever be drunk. It is the famous 'Bottle Museum', started as a tourist attraction by barman Perico Chicote in 1916 and now housed in new premises at the Plaza de Colon, Madrid.

The shelves of the museum are lined with 22,000 bottles, from 200 different countries, many of them bearing the names of distinguished donors. Between 'Ernest Hemingway' and H.M. Queen Soraya' is an inconspicuous visiting card which says, 'Perrott Phillips, Author'. It is propped up against a bottle of a particularly homicidal-looking spirit called *Konyagi*, from Tanzania.

It was my gift to Perico. The gesture was not altogether philanthropic. *Konyagi* has all the bouquet and distinction of napalm. I brought the bottle back from a holiday in East Africa, but no amount of guile or cunning could ever persuade my guests to touch the stuff. Appeals to their spirit of adventure fell on deaf ears. However riotous the party, one look at that label was enough to sober everyone up. After a thousand polite refusals, it has found its rightful home at last. Even though dinner parties will never be the same without that final, departure-inducing offer, 'Anyone for a drop of *Konyagi* before they go?'

Actually, with the exception of money and sex, more nonsense is talked about wine than any other subject. But sometimes a refreshing breeze blows through the cellar cobwebs. On a visit to a holiday camp in Devon, I enquired about the possibility of wine at dinner. 'Don't push it much these days, unless someone specifically asks,' said the manager resignedly, surveying the dining hall, where 600 people were tucking in at a furious rate. Apparently, they tried it once, placing bottles of white and red on every table before the guests arrived. The year was 1982 and the wine was labelled '1979'. It was too much for one of the happy campers. He waved the wine away, complaining, 'You're not getting *me* to drink up your old stock!'

For the no-nonsense approach, you need only turn to humorist Dorothy Parker, who was once persuaded to sample an evil home-made brew by her holiday hosts, who had converted their garden in Italy into a miniature vineyard.

'Where on earth does this wine come from?', she gasped, as the tannin ate into the enamel of her gritted teeth. 'From our own garden,' beamed her hosts, with all the smug self-satisfaction of home winemakers. 'Doesn't travel,' said Dorothy.

Dates to Remember

At last, the ultimate package tour. Moroccan docker Onri Larvi discovered it in 1983 when he took a lunchtime nap in a container on the dockside at Casablanca. As he slept, it was loaded aboard a ship bound for Spain. Larvi never gained the full benefit from the ports of call on his sixteen-day package cruise. The ship called at Cadiz, went on to Bilbao and then back to Cadiz before the container was opened and Larvi staggered out. He had survived on eight dates which had been left over from his lunch in Casablanca.

On Safari in SW7

If you have no sense of direction, take heart. Even the most intrepid traveller can get confused. Invited to dinner at the Geographical Club, a group of distinguished globetrotters set off from the Royal Geographical Society in Kensington Gore, London, just 400 yards away. Our heroes included travel-writer Brian Jackman, Sir Vivian Fuchs, President of the RGS, Dr John Hemmings, who knows the Amazon like the back of his hand, and Robin Hanbury-Tenison, who made the first land crossing of South America at its widest point. Within fifteen minutes, they were all hopelessly lost.

Not to Be Taken Internally

Getting into a country is often an obstacle race of visas, permits, Customs clearances and, in some cases, a £10 note slipped inside your passport. But in North Yemen, as *Daily Telegraph* correspondent John Bulloch discovered, the problem was getting out. Until he took his medicine.

Going from Sanaa to Saudi Arabia, he first had to get an exit visa. Then the Saudis insisted on a special 'health certificate' before they would grant it. The Yemen health department in turn decreed that a prescription they supplied must be obtained from a chemist before the certificate could be issued. At the pharmacy a bewildered Bulloch asked what the pills he had been given were for. 'For getting out of the country,' the chemist replied, with a perfectly straight face.

Sole Victim

One of the most remote areas of southern Spain is the Alpujarras, a mountain range which until recently had only barely been explored. One of the first people to open up the Alpujarras to serious travellers was Sally Harvey, who founded the horse-trekking company, *Aventura*. Planning one of the early horseback routes in the Alpujarras, Sally found herself alone in a deserted landscape, the only moving thing being her own shadow on the mountain trail. The track was fragile and difficult to follow but, if she stuck firmly to it, she could not go wrong. As mile succeeded mile, the track became narrower and more precipitous. But there was one encouraging sign; running ahead of her in the dust was the faint

but clear impression of tyremarks. 'If a motorbike can get up here,' Sally reasoned, 'so can I.' So she spurred her horse onwards and upwards, thinking of the chilled white wine at the end of the trail. Sally ended up perched on a terrifying peak with only two ways down, either straight over the cliff or back the way she had come. Quickly concluding that there was no future in equine hang-gliding as a sport, she turned round and retraced her steps, still puzzled at the tyremarks which had lured her all that way. It was not until she returned, exhausted, to the village where she had set off that she noticed a string of sandals hanging outside a little shop. Their soles were made of pieces of old motor-cycle tyre.

A Crash Course in Manglish

Ho, admirable perusers! In what ambience does the innovation all-speaking Manglish, help now of all tongues for easier leisure exploration of manykind, blossom to fullest flowering of rhapsodising aspirations? Answer me *that*, then.

If you have always wondered why Esperanto never really caught on, there is a simple answer. It has been superseded by Manglish, the true international language. Used almost exclusively by the authors of foreign tourist-guides and brochures, it could be mistaken at first sight for English, though its appeal crosses all linguistic frontiers. Unlike Esperanto, Manglish can achieve a strange, sometimes disconcerting, poetry of its own; an art form which succeeds in converting the humdrum and mundane into sheer fantasy.

An invitation to a shark-fishing trip, picked up in Tahiti, is a good example: 'Choice the best! Goo fortt ou Board my The shark fissing boat. Leef the harbour at 10am an have your fan, on board. A luxury 21m fissing boat, folly equiped for navigation. Roods reels baits and tuition by a very experimental crew. Return at 4pm after 6 hours of fan sun chaine relax and adventure.' What more could one want?

The humorist Paul Jennings possesses a recipe which came with a bottle of Italian olive oil and begins excitingly, 'Put the medal lions on the catlets, and small tomatoes. Stuff with caked Vegetable salad. Garish with chant.' But it is in the poetical-descriptive holiday brochure that Manglish really reveals its true potential for lyricism, unfettered by conventional rules of spelling, grammar, scansion or even sense. Take that wondrous *Guide to Lanzarote*, worth every penny of any poetry-lover's money, which gives the tiny Canary Island an unexpected aura of mystery:

> The stones of the monument as well as the coastal segment of Arrecife are loaded with history, and when you walk through the town at tepid nights, she comes towards you in unruly sensibility. Still embarrassed by the tremendous view of the kilometer wide masses of stones and lava, a light and corrupted wonder. As in other places that we have visited, we can watch women with their work and concentrate our look to the remarkable head protection to keep themselves off heat and wind. During a moment, we do not know where we are; in a village of senorial Castilla or in a town founded by the Vice-Kings of America . . . Chest of surprises that shelters in its interior the thousand years old crab.

Even the *Thousand-and-one Nights* sounds trite by comparison with the leaflet distributed by the Silver Casino and Cabaret, in Cairo: 'This Night Change the Story. And the Other Days. Casino and Cabaret Silver begin the Nighst Technical fine to B at Thursday dated 6 Juine, high memores men-logs Arabic and Europion players from famous Technical ladies & Twenty darling Fresh drinking nice complete service that Entre the satisfaction. To be past best sitting in engoying in Music sky showing the high life to whom shall come.'

Unlike many languages, Manglish succeeds in softening the edges of orders and instructions, which might sound curt in lesser tongues. In a letter to *The Observer*, Mrs Catherine Eyre quoted 'Hints to Campers' from a site in northern Italy:

> Peace is wished. Therefor art not allowed musicplaying, singing, using of radios, laud screams and yells, bambling of carrosseries, and so on . . . also have a thought for the sleaping people when it is 22pm, so dropp washing clothes or bits at that time, for the running water is noisy. Please protect the bushes, don't cut off trees or branches. Don't

build up wild walls of soncs or crabbs around your place. The stuff it is made of is blowen with the wind and disturbs everyone. Digging waterholes is not to do either. The one who does it has to planificate the spott before leaving. We wish to you a pleasurefull and peacefull subjurn. If you are in need of a help or feel like to slay up a wish, please you are welcome to us.

The longer the translation into Manglish, the more it loses contact with the prosaic. The result sometimes achieves a level of surrealism which would send James Joyce spinning merrily in his grave. You will not find Rodobaldo Aldama Adalia in any anthology of modern writing, which only shows how unfair the world can be. But if obscurity is the essence of original genius, you can imagine the awe with which tourists on the Costa Brava gazed at the notice he pinned up there in 1960:

EDICT
RODOBALDO ALDAMA ADALIA
The Jailer of Blanes Corporation

According to what has been disposed by the Minister of Government by circular, EVERYBODY MUST KNOW: To protect the most elemental norms of modesty and decency it is prohibited in all cases.
(1) The use of bath articles which be indecorous, demanding they cover the breast and shoulder as is due, being necessary they have skirts which are used by women and shorts by men.
(2) To remain in beaches, Clubs, cafes, restaurants and similar establishments, balls excursions, boats and generally, of watter-dressing bath suit, for his due use is into the water and one must only admit his veritable design.
(3) That men or women dress or undress in the beach, out-fermed cottage, to change the street suit or dress, by the bath suit and contrary.
(4) All nudity manifestations or incorrection in the same aspect, that not be in accord with Spanish traditional and good liking.
(5) Sun baths with moorish cloak untaken, our conditions thar are expressed in the following paragrapf.

Last norms must essentially be observed in the streets, beaches, river-shores, swimmingpools and other excursion places of local and amusement places, will be completed with the installation of 'solariums' which be covered, in which with the separation due of sexes and dressed with bath suit, to take sun-bathes will be allowed being necessary to go out the water snd remain in the 'solariums' the use of moorish cloaks which covered the body perfectly.

WHAT IS PUBLISHED TO BE KNOW AND ACCOMPLISHED

The Jailer

The work of Señor Adalia might well appear in O – level papers when Manglish belatedly becomes a compulsory language, as it must do eventually. Consider that last, resounding sentence, 'What is published is to be know and accomplished.' It is the kind of sage-like aphorism that has people nodding their heads gravely at cocktail parties. People have been interviewed in the literary pages of the *New York Times* for less.

A leaflet I picked up in Menorca captured the same mood of rhapsodic meaninglessness: 'Island of small size, but with great cariety of landscapes, and the visitor will enjoy discovering by himself so in villages, and in several places of coast, too. Main towns are ten, smiling, whites and harbourer, but each one with well definite characters.' In Italian hands, Manglish adopts a sprightlier, more outgoing tone, as in the brochure for the Palace-Hotel Lido in Cesenatico:

A squitt Italian and international Kitchen, best wines and a first class service you find in the hotel. Many rooms, you can luck on the sea. From the breakfasttable in the bathdress you doing on the beach. For your vanaces you have a place verry nice and indimenticabel.

71

The most telling translations start off cunningly by lulling you into thinking you are reading ordinary, workaday English. A paragraph later, you are up to the neck in the writer's stream of consciousness.

'Those who visit Viscaya will not find great monuments, majestic architecture or memories of events from a rather sensational past,' was the innocent start to a brochure on the Basque coast of France. From then on, it entered its own private world of imagery.

> Its inheritance while humble is both subtle and penetrating in that it graps the imagination of sensitive people and rivets ut an unspoiled frame for all the rest; its vorried vorcegated landscape of lights and shades is past the setting for a race which for so a long time has perplutated its close customs and language. The Basque coast is of more imprtance then the inland parts, and therefore more visitors and sperdy time over. It has a charm of its oun; wild, with the mountains nearing the sea, and the waves foamines on the rocks like wild horses, with manes flowires.

Wild horses, with 'manes flowires' or not, would not drag me to the Fiesta of San Fermin in Pamplona these days. Not since someone with a degree in Manglish published a *Guide to the Fiesta* so full of vague yet menacing warnings that even Ernest Hemingway would have drained his wineskin and fled back to Key West. 'VISITING TOURIST!' it starts, gripping you firmly by the lapels.

> WHAT YOU CAN DO FOR ST FERMIN. To form groups in order to manifest cheerfulness; taking instruments to give animation in the streets of the town; to direct people in the conditions as it ought to be with the adequate education to denote the correction and respect all the time; Intervention in the general ambient of the festivities presented in so far as it ought to be, that is, where personal clean clothing is concerned.

Do not think you can wriggle free yet. While you are still worrying whether you can manifest enough cheerfulness – or whether your clothes are clean enough to satisfy the authorities – the *Guide* now proceeds to lecture you on:

72

WHAT YOU MUST NOT DO FOR ST FERMIN. To walk around alone or in groups, in an inadequate form and adapting attitudes that denote a personal bad state, to offend elemental civil conduct. To sit down or lie down in the sight of the public, to obstruct the freedom and movement of people. To break or tear objects in sight of the public or crowded places. Running or staying in the running of the bulls in an intoxicated state, or appearing in inadequate clothing. To hold down and to hit the cows and bulls in Bull Square or in the bull ring.

Now go out and enjoy yourself.

Rather less threatening in tone, but equally disorientating, is the official guide to the Gascon resort of Anglet, which begins by painting an idyllic picture:

> Whoever has come as yet has always enjoyed the boundless flirting of the sun with the sea all along the sands of its three miles shore, the brightly-faceted ocean with the healthy spray of its gentle breath. Would you rather indulge in quiet resting? Or have you sudden mind to golf. Just bend your steps inwards and links await you; with a few more steps you may as well encounter some of the riders.

But suddenly the theme curdles:

> Anglet cherichses its past and the Gascon folklore actually achieves its customary truculence with the famous cowfighting and the tricks performed by the so-called fighters who do nothing but play with small and nervy cows. So whatever your tastes, and may you be fond of being alone or squashed within the madding crowd, you will find in Anglet what you may be looking for. And after you have discovered it, you will surely keep repeating for a long time.

Where Manglish falls down is in exposition. The vocabulary, even in the hands of a master, is not suited to the brief, lucid explanation. A brochure writer who tried to explain the origin of the words *Via de la Plata* – the name of an historic seventeenth-century hotel in Merida, Spain – found himself out of his depth within the first sentence.

> The Kilometre 'O' on the way of the Argent road is in Merida and goes along Caceres, Salamanca, Zamora and ends at Astorga. Roman road that I say at first, it begins in this Augusta Emerita and with every roman construction is the admiration of all future civilisations up to the present time. Ways, bridges, theatres are the whole of an Empire and it wonder us. The name of this road is up to date a small mistery and we could atribute it to Arabs peoples with the construction of the word BALAT: pavement, it is, way, they wanted to appoint it with the best way, as a manner of admiration for roman people. It is wrong to atribute this name to the argent transport in this for roman people.

So now you know.

This is not to say that the inspired user of Manglish cannot achieve a stunning effect in only a few words. I remember the impact on passing British tourists caused by four posters advertising a forthcoming dance, pasted side by side on a wall in Palma, Majorca. To make it a truly international affair, the posters were in Spanish, French, German and English. 'Baile! Baile! Baile!' trumpeted the Spanish version. 'Tanze! Tanze! Tanze!' boomed the German. 'Dance! Dance! Dance!' proclaimed the French. 'Balls! Balls! Balls!' hooted the Manglish.

French Connection

The Ritz Hotel in London was left, not with egg, but champagne on its face when it sent out 12,000 leaflets offering discount terms during the low season, plus a bottle of bubbly for every guest. All you had to do was telephone their number. The stunt worked like a charm and the switchboard was jammed with eager tourists. Sadly, it was Air France's freephone switchboard. The handout had got the hotel phone number wrong by one digit, resulting in a perplexed Air France team trying to make sense of hundreds of people demanding what the hotel had described as 'A special blend of hospitality . . .'

Light Relief

A distinguished executive on British Caledonian Airways (who must be protected by anonymity) was driving through Kampala, in Uganda, when he accidently skimmed past a black policeman who was holding up the oncoming traffic at an intersection. The policeman leaped from his little platform, his face contorted with rage, and hammered on the bonnet of the car with his truncheon, demanding furiously, 'What colour do you think I am?' There are times when, whatever you say, it is going to be the wrong thing and the executive from BCAL did not intend to take any chances. He had read Konrad Lorenz's books on the territorial imperative and he knew exactly what move to make next. He got out of the car, smiled, spread his hands and bowed his head in what he hoped was a suitably apologetic, contrite and self-abasing manner. It did not satisfy the policeman. 'What colour am I?' he repeated, whacking the car again and inflicting a nasty dent in the No Claims Bonus. The BCAL man's colour was now only too clear, ashen. He knew he must make no reference whatsoever, however conciliatory, to the policeman's skin, which left him with no alternative. 'I am afraid, constable', he replied lamely, and in a voice like a breaking twig, 'I don't know.' Immediately, the policeman struck a commanding pose, with his hand held high. 'When I do this', he said, 'I am red.' Then he beckoned with his other hand at an imaginary motor car. 'When I do *this*, I am green!'

Asking for Trouble

The violinist, Fritz Kreisler, was walking down 5th Avenue, New York, his mind fixed on his next concert, when he was stopped by a tourist, map in hand. 'How do I get to Carnegie Hall?' asked the man. 'Practise, practise, practise,' said Kreisler, hurrying on. An elevated reply, and a far whack of the truncheon from the British tourist, also lost in New York, who asked a patrolman the way to the Empire State Building. 'Don't bother me, Mac,' snapped the officer, 'I've got problems of my own!' considerably ruffled, the Briton said stiffly, 'Thank *you*.' 'You're welcome,' replied the policeman.

Have Gun, Will Travel

Television presenters who try to throw their weight around with film crews on foreign assignments get cut down to size with merciless speed. One of the most arrogant of TV frontmen (the one who appears on your screen in para-military uniform, usually shouting above the roar of helicopters) became so unpopular with his crew that they devised a practical joke of quite devilish simplicity. One of the crew cut the outline of a pistol from a sheet of metal foil. Just before the presenter reached the security check at a particularly sensitive Middle East airport, the cutout was slipped between the pages of a newspaper in his hand baggage. The tele-person stood innocently by as his case slid into the X-ray machine. The next moment there was pandemonium. Security guards, police and trigger-itchy soldiers appeared from nowhere. The presenter was pinned to the wall, speechless with bewilder-

ment, as guards tore through his clothes and his case was ripped to pieces before his eyes. It took ages – amid threats of electric shock torture by the police and hysterical protestations of innocence by the tele-person – before the tinfoil cut-out was discovered. The security men did not exactly fall about laughing; but the presenter, at least, had learned humility.

Odd Signs and Even Odder Notices

They seek him here, they seek him there. The Demon Signwriter of the Sahara. Not much call for signs in the Sahara, you may think, but you would be wrong. Scattered along the Tunisian rim of the desert are a few 'last chance' cafes and hotels, bursting to advertise their amenities to the occasional camel caravan. It is here that the Demon Signwriter finds his victims.

I first stumbled across his handiwork at Chebika, a tiny oasis almost smothered in sand. The Demon had persuaded a gullible native that business would boom beyond all dreams of avarice if he had the word 'Cafe' written in four languages on the side of his modest shack. You could tell the poor chap had been conned. His body hunched in glum resignation, he sat moodily beneath the finished sign:

Cafe

Cafe

Cafe

Kafe

The slight concession towards the German language in the word 'Kafe' was intriguing. Was it a clue? The same cunning hand had been at work in the oasis at Tamerza, a few miles further on. This time the Demon Signwriter had sold the word 'Reception' to the owner of a small, wood-frame guest house. The result was the same. Outside the box-like lobby, in the usual four languages, were the words:

Reception

Reception

Reception

Rezeption

Adolf Hitler used to be a signwriter. Was this the biggest news scoop of the twentieth century? His moustache bleached white in the Saharan sun, was the Führer still alive, wandering the desert with brush and paintpot, surviving feebly on his only remaining talent? No way of telling. As

Omar Khayam almost wrote, 'The moving finger cons, and having conned, moves on.'

All over the world, signs are proliferating. They breed at night, I'm sure. No traveller can take a step without being ordered to do this, that or the other. Not to go in, not to go out, not to wander about without a guide, not to hire unofficial guides, not to go hatless, not to go topless, not to go naked, not to cross the grass, not to swim, not to fish, not to spit, not to talk to the driver while the coach is in motion.

The most arresting sign was spotted by a group of tourists passing through Marbella. A banner stretched right across the front of a newly finished apartment block offered, 'LUXURY CONDOMS FOR SALE'.

Not all notices have the whimsical sense of humour of those at Nairobi Serpent Park in Kenya. The park houses a wide variety of venomous snakes, but visitors are far more likely to die laughing than choking. 'Tresspassers will be

poisoned', warns the notice pinned on wire netting separating you from a spaghetti-junction of cobras. Another says pointedly, 'Visitors throwing litter into the crocodile pit will be required to retrieve it.'

The most devious notice of all is pinned on the door of the curator's office:

WARNING TO VISITORS
Snakes are often allowed loose in
this office to have the poison
removed from their fangs. You enter
at your own risk.

Whether he feels like brewing the odd cup of tea, or settling down to a good book, the curator can smile to himself, sure of one thing. He will not be disturbed by unwelcome callers.

Slightly less droll, but in the same spirit, is the sign outside Colombo Zoo, Sri Lanka:

If you litter with disgrace
and spoil the beauty of this place
May indigestion rack your chest
and ants invade your pants and vest.

No, the general tone of signs and notices directed at visitors the world over is usually incivil, abrupt, hectoring or sinister.

For the maximum disquiet in the minimum number of words, the notice greeting arrivals at Changi Airport, Singapore, takes some beating: *WARNING! The penalties for importing drugs are severe, including death.* 'Including' is a very unsettling word to use when referring to capital punishment. Are there other penalties, so horrific that the notice dare not even hint at them? The mind boggles.

After a menacing warning like that, it is a relief to return to the well-meaning, slightly fey signs one encounters in rural England, that haven of eccentricity.

There is more than a touch of Alice in Wonderland about the sign in Yorkshire which says merely, 'Do not throw stones at this sign.' In Bexhill there is a sign which just says, 'Please do not lean cycles against this sign.' In Carlisle, another whose only words are, 'Not to be removed.' All of them pointers to a lost world of innocence.

Sir Roy Strong, Director of the Victoria and Albert Museum, spotted the most patrician sign of them all while taking a bath in one of our statelier homes. 'Please do not let the bath overflow,' it said civilly. 'The Michelangelo is in the room below.'

In the realms of the unreal, there is, of course, nothing to touch the names of British business partners, as advertised by signboards above estate agents, lawyers and accountants' offices. How on earth did the solicitor Lyer ever meet, in a million years of coincidence, such a perfectly named partner as Phibbs? Yet there they are, linked forever in litigation, in northern Ireland. The same goes for the wondrous trio, with offices in Ludgate Circus, London, 'Stray, Clogg and Alabaster'. The estate agents 'Bacchus and Gathercole' (are they animal, mineral or mythological?) disport themselves in deepest Surrey. And in Lower Thames Street, in the City of London, are the magical furriers, 'Garfunkel and Wanderer'. I always imagine dauntless Wanderer, dressed in a huge fur coat and coonskin hat, dragging his sledge through a Siberian blizzard in search of mink and sable, while stooped old Garfunkel minds the till back home.

Russian signs have an exotic magic all their own, probably due to the Cyrillic alphabet, like the word PECTOPAH, which most tourists pronounce phonetically, not knowing that the actual pronounciation is, simply, 'Restaurant'.

On the other hand, the warning in a Leningrad hotel that 'Ladies are requested not to have children in the bar', does *not* mean exactly what it says.

During a visit to Siberia, the executive editor of the *Daily Telegraph*, Jeremy Deedes, was mystified by the manifestly English word 'Vauxhall' displayed in huge red letters across the front of the railway station at Khabarovsk. A local guide supplied the answer. Before the Russians built their first railway stations, they sent a team of engineers to England to see how they worked. Vauxhall Station, in London, was then regarded as a showpiece and the visiting Russians spent weeks studying its layout. Unfortunately, nobody explained to them that Vauxhall was a place. The Russians thought the word meant 'station'. Which is why, believe it or not, all Russian stations have the unlikely name, Vauxhall.

When they are not totally incomprehensible, American notices tend to be either strident (*Walk! Don't Walk!* are the marching-orders on traffic lights) or humourless, sometimes both at the same time. A perfect example is the aggressively feminist coffee-shop in Cambridge, Massachusetts, which, appalled at the sexist implications of the words Waiter and Waitress, instructs its customers to call them 'Waitrons'.

Americans also hesitate to use one word when ten will do; which explains the sign on the door of a department store at

Clearwater, Florida. 'The functioning quality of this exit is now deleted.' Or as you and I would say, 'Closed'. Heavens knows how many British motorists in the United States have been mystified (sometimes to bursting point) by the common motorway sign, 'Rest Area Ahead. No Rest Rooms'. And spare a tear for the thousands of children whose belief in Father Christmas must have been rudely shattered by the banner outside a New York department store which read, 'Five Santas. No waiting.'

The quintessential American sign winks naughtily above a sleazy peepshow joint off Broadway in San Francisco. On and off goes the scarlet invitation, 'Talk to a Naked Girl, $1.' For nearly a month, while filming a TV programme there, I watched that sign flutter wickedly. My colleagues speculated lewdly and endlessly on what line of conversation to pursue for $1. Like Oscar Wilde, I can resist anything except temptation, so I was the one who eventually went in, dollar in hand. So just what *do* you say to an unclothed hooker before the steel shutter comes down after thirty seconds? (That is the catch, to carry on talking you need a further supply of dollars). The stitchless lady, who looked as if she had heard every obscene suggestion known to man or beast, waited resignedly.

'I would like to begin where I left off yesterday', I said brightly, 'discussing the middle-European *zeitgeist* represented by the decline of the Austro-Hungarian empire and its influence on the music of Gustav Mahler . . .'

Her look of bemused disbelief will remain with me to my dying day.

Service Charge

Holidaymakers who may have noticed a sudden and dramatic improvement in service in Indonesia should thank the government's new Incentives Scheme. Anyone obstructing tourists will now be executed. 'The quality of service given to foreign tourists at airports, seaports and hotels was low, and sometimes obstacles were put in their way,' admitted Selman Harjowisastro, the Director of Tourist Travel Development, early in 1985. Now for the good news. 'In future, the government will treat people who obstruct the tourist programme as subversives.' The maximum penalty for subversion is death.

Bedroom Farce

And so to the Misunderstanding of the Year Award. An Indian couple visiting Edinburgh bought two balcony seats for the play, *A Bedful of Foreigners*. During the interval, according to *The Scotsman*, they returned in a highly confused state to the foyer, saying that there seemed to be some mistake. They thought they had booked into an hotel.

Do They Mean U.S.?

British social life is full of subtle hints and inflections and fear of making a *faux pas* can often trip up the unwary tourist. Couple that with a nervousness about our ritual and traditions and you have yawning in front of you a positive minefield of potential embarrassment. Taking a party of Americans through the House of Commons, a guide suddenly spotted Mr Neil Kinnock, the Leader of the Labour Party, whom he knew well. 'Neil!' he exclaimed, at which point all the Americans dropped to their knees.

Innocent seekers after culture that they are, Americans do tend to get things a trifle confused. A British Tourist Association guide was cornered by a New Yorker with little time to spare who demanded to see Gray's Elegy. When she explained that he couldn't see the elegy because it was a poem, but they were going to visit Stoke Poges churchyard where it was composed, the American's response was less than enthusiastic. 'We don't want to see any more * * * churches,' he fumed, 'We just want to see a * * * elegy!' the same guide overheard a woman from Minneapolis, who telescoped several centuries in a few words after toiling up the hill to the terrace of Edinburgh Castle. 'Mary Queen of Scahts must have been plumb crazy to build up here', she panted. 'It's so far from the shops.'

As for Stonehenge, there are visitors who actually seem to think that it is a holiday hotel the Druids never got round to finishing. 'Hasn't changed much since 1972, has it?' an American woman was heard to comment in 1985. This observation reminded me of the courier of a group from Chicago being shown round the Roman Colosseum a few months before Italy was due to host the 1968 Olympics. As one man clambered down, he turned sorrowfully to his guide and said, 'I'm a builder and I hate to have to say this, but you'll never have it ready in time for the Games.'

An American visitor to Cirencester's Corinium Museum, which has some of the finest Roman exhibits in Britain, was equally hazy about the past. Gazing at a beautifully preserved mosaic, he shook his head sadly and said, 'It must have been a lovely picture before it was smashed into all those little pieces.'

My personal prize for sublime historical disregard is awarded without hesitation to the elderly American couple I encountered in the ruins of Luxor. It was the last day of a long and demanding cruise down the Nile, during which we had seen wonderful things. 'How's it going?' I asked. In the shadow of one of mankind's grandest creations, the husband looked at me bleakly and replied, 'We'll be glad to get back to civilisation.'

Chopin Spree

It takes a lot to overawe a crowd who are determined to enjoy themselves, and a typically robust spirit was displayed by a group of north 'of England tourists being conducted sombrely through the famous monastery at Valldemosa, in Mallorca, where Chopin once spent a thoroughly dismal winter with his mistress, George Sand. While some were still speculating over George's gender ('Ee, was that Chopin *gay?*'), the party reached the most revered relic in the monastery, the piano on which the master is said to have composed several major works in the winter of 1839. Nodding sagely, as if back in Workington they did little else but whistle Chopin, the visitors filed past. Just as the head of the queue left the room, the respectful calm was shattered by a cheerful jangling. One of the party had vaulted the rope barrier and was merrily banging out *Yessir, that's my baby* on the piano. 'I only wanted to liven up the place a bit,' were her last words as attendants, helped by two burly monks, led her away to the delighted cheers of her friends.

Waiter, there's a Corpse in my Soup

Eat it, enjoy it, but never ever try to identify it. That is the best advice when confronted with a suspicious-looking dish plucked at random from the kind of foreign menu where the only decipherable item is the name of the manager.

Please do not take my word for it. Ask food writer Bill Vine, who made the mistake of enquiring too closely into some meat balls, dipped in honey, served at a banquet in

YOUR MEAL WILL BE HERE SHORTLY

Hong Kong. Turning to his Chinese host, Bill asked brightly what type of meat he had just eaten and enjoyed. A bad move. The Chinaman searched for the right words and then replied, 'How you say in English . . . little white mices?'

Not surprisingly, I have learned to distrust far-flung foreign restaurants. Not that I am a namby-pamby eater, far from it. I would order anything from a menu except the waiter's thumbprint.

I did not turn a hair when they poured black rum and pepper on my clam chowder in Bermuda. I have sampled snake soup in China, 'Cobra coffee' in Bombay and even 'Sea slug in crab grease' on Penang. In a native beerhall on the outskirts of Nairobi, I clenched my teeth and sipped 'Kaffir beer', which looked like porridge and tasted like Polycell wallpaper paste. Nor did I go green in Korea, when every dish on the menu ended with the word 'yuk'. It is, you will be relieved to know, Korean for 'meat'. And who was the only one to order 'Stuffed Pussy' in a highly embarrassed group at the Green Parrot Restaurant on St Lucia? It was avocado filled with flaked cod.

British restaurants, of course, have their own little refinements. A *Good Food Guide* inspector reported visiting a dire restaurant where the patron, after being deserted by his staff, dropped the grouse he was serving. He promptly picked it up and offered it at half price 'because it only just touched the floor'.

One of the few places in Europe where you really know where you are, gastronomically speaking, is Oslo. No nonsense there about which restaurant to choose or whether it will live up to Michelin's little galaxies of stars. As you leave the airport, you are handed a 100–page guide to 'Where to Eat in Oslo'. Whatever page you turn to, it bears the single recommendation 'Restaurant Lidvink'. Visitors cannot make up their minds whether it is a gag, a typographical error of epic proportions or a brilliant publicity stunt. Either way, the Restaurant Lidvink is full every night.

I wish things had been as simple in Washington DC, where I once took a girl-friend into a restaurant rather laboriously decked out as a Wild West saloon. It was called something macho, like 'Bunfight at the OK Corral', so it was a surprise when the epicene Maitre'd took exception to my companion's trouser suit. 'No pants allowed!' he lisped firmly, ushering us back into the street with ill-concealed distate. More than somewhat ruffled, I put on my best David Niven voice, called for the manager and insisted on being admitted, pointing out that trouser-suits happened to be the latest fashion in a dowdy little backwater called London. Grudgingly, we were stuck behind a pillar far from the outraged sensibilities of the other diners; only to be served a few moments later by a topless waitress.

The First Law of Gastronomics, I have found, is: The quality of the food is always in inverse ratio to the height of the restaurant. With few exceptions, the higher you go in those 'Top o'the Tower' type restaurants, the worse the food becomes; and if it revolves as well, then the first victim of the Revolution is the cuisine.

There was a bizarre evening in a revolving rooftop restaurant in the Caribbean, when something went wrong with the mechanism and the help-yourself buffet started to draw away from us like a carnival float. By the time we got to our second course – and were admiring the view from the wrap-around window – the entire buffet had revolved out of sight round the other side of the tower.

To anguished cries of 'Follow that buffet!' we leaped from our tables to the inner ring carrying the runaway food, waving our plates like a demonstration of Greek discus-throwers. We never caught up with our sherry trifle. We were carried backwards, gesticulating helplessly, as if we had stepped on an airport travelator going in the wrong direction.

A famous British journalist, of completely spherical appearance and messy eating habits, used to reappear from his travels with the cuisine of the country tastefully arranged all over his tie. It told us instantly where he had been. 'Ah, just back from Valencia, eh Arthur?' we would say, as the unmistakeable whiff of paella drifted up from his Paisley-pattern neckwear.

I stopped scoffing at Arthur the day I was forced to eat the tablecloth at Addis Abbaba. My host had taken me to what he described as 'a typical Ethiopian restaurant' in the dingy and labyrinthine back streets of the capital. We sat at a bare wickerwork table and consulted the menu, which consisted basically of only one dish, *njera* and *wot*. My misgivings were not dispelled by the appearance of *tej*, an Ethiopian spirit with all the subtlety of paraquat, which was poured by the waiter from what was clearly an old and barely recycled Johnnie Walker bottle.

The ordeal had only just begun. Over the table the waiter spread a grey cloth made of some thick and spongy material like foam rubber. The absence of cutlery, even plates, should have made me suspicious. A moment later, he reappeared with a large tureen of some glutinous, stew-like substance and promptly emptied it into the middle of the table. In disbelief, I watched my host tear a chunk off the tablecloth, wrap a handful of the stew in it and shove it into his mouth, with every sign of satisfaction. The tablecloth, a kind of unleavened bread, was the *njera*. The stew was the *wot*.

As I reached out to copy him, he laid a gentle hand on my arm. 'It is customary in my country for the host to feed the guests,' he smiled. At first I did not catch on. But as I opened my mouth to say 'Oh, really?' he grabbed another handful of the stew-and-tablecloth and rammed it into my mouth. For the next two hours, every time I opened my mouth to speak, the black hand would flash out with another cheek-bulging load of *njera* and *wot*. All I can say is I have discovered the ultimate conversation-stopper.

I only ever heard of one dish more heave-making. The distinguished foreign correspondent, John Deane Potter, once swore to me that he had been forced to eat some fibrous root in an African kraal, each piece of which had already been chewed by the tribal chief as a mark of respect to the guest.

Sang froid is a vital requirement in the professional traveller. For Conspicuous Gallantry in the Face of Enemy Food, the Gastronomic VC must go to the reporter, Donald Wise, then of the *Daily Express*.

Wise was eating at a pavement cafe during the Algerian civil war when a dead soldier – picked off by a sniper's bullet – crashed from an overhead window on to his table. 'Excuse me, waiter,' he said, raising one elegant finger, 'There's a dead man in my soup.'

There is no accounting for taste, as a bishop discovered when he attended a banquet given by Queen Mary at Badminton during World War Two. It was the then Queen Mother's habit to reward her favourite dog with a biscuit at the end of a meal. Assuming that the Bishop knew all about this little ritual, she handed it to him with all the regal *hauteur* she possessed – which was considerable – but, unfortunately, without a word of explanation. Instead of passing it on to the slavering Corgi under the table, the bishop interpreted the gesture as a special, if somewhat eccentric, mark of favour and doggedly chewed his way through the biscuit right down to the last crumb.

The occasional dog-biscuit never did anyone any harm; the British Navy lived on them for centuries. Though I dread to think what went into the stockpot of the restaurant I spotted in Valencia called El Botulin, and the mind boggles (not to

WAITER!

speak of the stomach) at the after-effects of a meal at the Trattoria Salmonella, in Palermo.

A friend who foolishly enquired in a Dublin eatery, 'What are the shrimps like, waiter?' got the instant reply, 'Sure, dey're tiny pink t'ings, like your little finger, sor.'

And entering a restaurant in The Gambia, West Africa, is venturing into a world where nothing is what it seems. Not that it is easy to find a restaurant outside the excellent ones in the hotels. In the shanty-town capital, Banjul, there is just

91

one, a surrealist place decorated like a German bier-keller and serving German specialities. Well, almost. Feeling in the mood for a plateful of typical *Deutsches Kuchen* one evening, the TV producer James Pople sat down and ordered the frankfurter and sauerkraut. The waiter looked distinctly uneasy. Glancing furtively from side to side, he whispered, 'I wouldn't have the frankfurter if I were you, sir. Try the Bockwurst instead.' 'Why?' Pople enquired, in all innocence. 'Because the Bockwurst only comes from Las Palmas,' explained the waiter. 'Then where on earth do the German frankfurters come from?' Pople pressed on. 'Dakar,' said the waiter bleakly.

Holidaymaker Mr Mark Dixon also expected something better when he went into the well-known P. J. Clarke restaurant in New York. He was rapidly disillusioned when he discovered his salad was garnished by an odd ingredient, a cockroach. Far from apologising profusely and whipping the dish away, the head waiter adopted an arrogant tone. 'Sir,' he told Mr Dixon, 'if you continue to draw so much attention to what is, after all, only *one* cockroach, I will have to ask you to leave this restaurant.' As Mr Dixon wrote to *The Times*, 'A New York restaurant must be the only place where the customer is escorted to the door and not the cockroach.'

Mrs Margaret Cavendish got more than she bargained for when she wandered into a small bar in Competa, a remote village in southern Spain, where a notice proclaimed, 'Special today, *Ranas*.' Obviously, it was not an opportunity to be missed, but what exactly were they? The barman was none too helpful. '*Ranas*,' he explained, making a crablike movement across the bar with his hand. 'Crab?' ventured Mrs Cavendish. 'No, no,' he replied, '*ranas*.' This time he flapped his elbows like a bird. 'Some sort of bird?' queried Mrs Cavendish. 'No,' he repeated impatiently, '*ranas*,' and opened and closed his mouth like a goldfish. Was it a fish? The final question seemed to send the barman crazy. He leaped from behind the bar, crouched on the floor and to

everyone's astonishment started hopping around, croaking wildly. Before the men in white coats came to take him away, the penny dropped. *Ranas* was Spanish for frogs.

Only once have I ever got the better of a restaurant, and that was in a painfully pretentious place in Estepona, on the Costa del Sol, where all the walls are lined with movie stills and the dishes are named after film stars. I settled for the Steak Frank Sinatra. 'How would you like it done?' asked the waiter. 'My waaaaay!' I sang out, in a passable imitation of Ole Blue Eyes himself. There are some opportunities in life one just cannot resist; and that little *jeux d'esprit* was one of them.

Relative Misunderstanding

Never look a gift slave in the mouth. When Dr Roger Sawyer was in the Sahara in 1984, researching his book *Slavery in the Twentieth Century*, his interpreter took him to visit a relative who lived in a small village. During the conversation Dr Sawyer mentioned that he was interested in the welfare of children. The relative misunderstood him completely and immediately offered him a seven-year-old girl, adding, 'This is one of my slaves. You are welcome to her.' Refusing as politely as he could, Dr Sawyer only succeeded in making matters worse. 'What I meant to say', he explained, 'is that girls are better off with their mothers.' Whereupon the mother was promptly added to the gift.

Naked Ambition

Granted the possibility of reincarnation, many men would like to return as ski instructors; combining as they do healthy exercise, undisputed authority and overwhelming sexual attration in a quite insufferable form. All this is pure envy, of course, but some hint of the heady lifestyle of the average ski instructor was given by Oliver Denton, describing his experiences in *Travelling* magazine. One winter, while he was teaching at Chamonix, a group of Physical Education girls arrived from Sweden, including a blonde Amazon who could easily have doubled for Brunhilde. On the last night of their holiday, she challenged Oliver to the traditional *coureur nus*, or 'naked runner' dare. Basically, this involves hurtling down the piste in the nude, normally at night for the sake of modesty. Oliver accepted the challenge, with the girl making the sole condition that she made the first run, and alone. On the night, the Amazon went to the far end of the piste, stripped off her clothes and handed them to a friend to take down to the finishing line. Although it is never completely dark in the Alps – the snow reflects the slightest sliver of moonlight – the girl chose her moment to come down when the clouds had just scudded across the moon. The eager audience was left with little more than the impression of a hurtling silhouette as she completed the quarter-mile run. At the finishing line, next to the car park, her friends immediately formed a circle round her as she dressed. And now it was Oliver's turn. Taking his cue from the girl, he waited until the moon slid once more behind the clouds, then rocketed down at a speed which would have impressed Franz Klammer. Just a hundred yards from the end, and still a sexless blur to the spectators, he saw the girl make a sudden signal with her arm. At that moment, all the cars in the car-park switched on their headlights at full beam, catching him in a dazzling spotlight. No skier ever had a more dramatic or revealing finish.

Whine, Women and Song

You just can't please some package tourists, as anyone who handles their complaints will tell you. Horizon Holidays once published a selection of comments from less-than-satisfied customers which disproved for ever the idea that travel broadens the mind. Funny Foreign Food came top of the hit-list, with one customer complaining, 'If I had been the chef, I would have put my head in the dustbin along with the other fish heads.' Presumably talking from experience, another commented, 'The food is better in prison and you get longer to eat it.' One terrible shock for tourists was that Abroad is full of foreigners. 'The hotel itself spoke little or no English', whinged one client, 'and was full of Spanish-type French people.' And there was obviously no satisfying the holidaymaker who claimed that 'To play tennis at night, one had to have luminous balls.' A Cosmos Holidays executive once told me about a woman who asked for a refund when she returned from Majorca because, 'Although you promised in the brochure that all rooms had TV, I was only able to get Spanish-speaking programmes.' For splendid ambiguity, however, there is no beating the man who wrote to a tour operator complaining about the food in Greece, 'It wasn't fit for pigs. And the portions were too small, as well.'

Going for Broke

Yard for yard, moving house is fraught with more peril than any other form of travel. A firm named Amertrans, which specialises in removals to the United States, boasts that 'We never break anything' – a claim which was taken up with relish by one customer, with the promise, 'If you smash just one item, I'll sue, sue, sue!' The packers knew a veiled hint when they heard one and treated every one of her possessions with kid gloves. Imagine their chagrin when unpacking at the other end to find a shelf made of expensive bevelled glass cracked obviously and irreparably in two. Enter the sales manager in a puff of green smoke. He knew he had exactly two hours' grace before the woman got back to the house and they had to own up to the breakage. With great presence of mind, he skimmed through the Yellow Pages of the local telephone directory and found (a) a glass supplier (b) a specialist who silvered mirrors and (c) a firm that bevelled glass. Pleading, wheedling and cajoling, he somehow co-ordinated all three together to produce an exact replica of the broken shelf within two hours. The price was extortionate but the company's reputation was saved. 'And last, but not least', said the packers, unable to resist the temptation when the woman turned up, 'here is the last item to be unwrapped safe and sound, your mirror shelf.' 'Funny,' said the woman, genuinely bemused, 'as long as I've known it, there has been a crack down the middle.'

Lost for Words

A taxi-driver who speaks English, and can double as an interpreter, is an essential part of any foreign correspondent's equipment. Fluency is not expected; indeed, it is important to keep conversations basic enough to avoid misunderstanding. Michael Parkinson discovered this the hard way when he was sent to Turkey to cover a delicate situation involving Greece. Parkinson succeeded in setting up a television interview with a high-ranking Turkish official, only to find out the man spoke no English. Since Parkinson's Turkish was only vestigial, this did not augur well for clarity of communication, until he thought of letting his taxi-driver, who spoke both Turkish and English, sit in as interpreter. On the director's call of 'Action!' Parkinson asked the official to summarise the state of affairs existing between Greece and Turkey. The cabbie translated, the official looked suitably thoughtful and then delivered a ten-minute answer, couched in placatory terms and full of diplomatic niceties. When he ended, Parkinson turned to his driver for the translation. The cabbie pondered a moment and then said, 'Boss, he says we're gonna kick the sheet out of each other.'

Our Hotel's an Absolute Hole

Wandering innocently near the reception area of a London hotel, a bewildered guest was suddenly pounced on by the hotelier, manhandled into the kitchen and ordered to wash up a huge pile of plates. 'Your first day at work here', screamed the hotelier as he stormed out, 'and you're late!' How was the poor guest to know that he had been mistaken for a kitchen hand who was due to start that day?

An everyday story of hotel folk, as published in the *Daily Telegraph* Peterborough column. No wonder that, when it first started, I thought *Fawlty Towers* was a documentary. Surely every hotel is like that. And aren't all hoteliers neurotic despots, and their guests totally barmy?

A television team filming at the Railway Hotel in York thought they had stumbled on a News at Ten story when fire engines, ambulances and a police car hurtled to a halt at the door. It transpired that one of the guests had gone mad, painted his entire room with glue and papered over all the doors and windows. The first the management heard of it was when he phoned down to reception with a rambling story about a conspiracy to pump poison gas into his room. 'But I've beaten them!' he cackled, as the desk clerk dialled 999.

Another London hotelier told about the loopy couple from California who announced each morning, 'Today we are expecting a phone call from the Queen, inviting us to tea at Buckingham Palace. If we are out, please take the message.'

Breathless, the couple would rush back from their sightseeing and ask, 'Did *she* telephone?' After two weeks of this, the staff felt they had almost become part of the same fantasy-world and had to restrain themselves from saying, 'Yes, an equerry will be meeting you in the State Carriage at ten tomorrow morning and a troop of mounted Life Guards will escort you to the Palace . . .' The couple returned to California, convinced that only high affairs of State had prevented the Queen finding time for them.

All London hoteliers know that foreigners regard our police as fairy godmothers whose sole duty is to protect them from greedy and dishonest innkeepers. One Iranian called the police from his room because there were nylon instead of cotton sheets on the bed. And at the same hotel, a German rushed down the stairs shouting, 'Polizei, call ze Polizei!' Apparently, the water in his room was not hot enough.

Mr Len Maddocks, who runs the exemplary Empire Hotel in Llandudno, always steels himself before telling English guests that every room has a bath. It is amazing how many get ruffled and reply, almost indignantly, 'We've already *had* a bath, thank you very much.'

Just how Mr Maddock's guests would react to the novel hotel 'plumbing' discovered by Michael Parkinson, the TV chat-show host, is anyone's guess. 'It was at a French-run holiday village near Goreme, in Turkey', he said. 'On the first morning, I climbed out of bed and turned on the tap. To my surprise, the water came out bright red. I filled a glass and sipped it. It was red wine. The other tap? White wine.'

As part of the holiday spirit, running *rouge* and *blanc* had been piped to every bedroom, making it the only place where you could get pie-eyed just by cleaning your teeth.

In all seriousness, a British hotel manager once commented, 'The snag with running a hotel is having to accommodate guests. If we didn't have so many, the whole place would run more smoothly.'

In a recent court case, a young couple described how they arrived at a Spanish hotel, to be greeted by an angry manager wielding a baseball bat and holding back a snarling Alsatian. 'The manager seemed to think we were burglars', said the young man. 'It wasn't until we showed him our passports and spent ten minutes arguing with him that he let us in.' Have you ever had the feeling you're not wanted?

A magazine competition to find 'The Hotel of the Year' in 1986 inspired almost as many entries telling the other side of the story. Arriving in New York after midnight, Mr Peter George, of Gomshall, Surrey, finally found a hotel with vacancies. Reaching his room, he had trouble with the light switch, so made his way over to the bed and sat on it while trying to get the bedside lamp to work. The bed seemed a bit lumpy. Once the light went on, he discovered he was sitting on a corpse. Recovering from the shock, he went down to the lobby and said to the bored receptionist, 'I'd like to change my room, because there seems to be a dead man in the bed.' The clerk did not even look up, but simply swivelled his chair to get a new key and said, 'Okay, Mac, you're now in Room 201.'

Fast asleep at the International Hotel in Prague, Mr Melville Summerfield, from Gosforth, Newcastle upon Tyne, was abruptly woken at 6 a.m. by an alarm call he had not booked. When he complained, the receptionist agreed but explained that the person next door had booked an early-morning call, and as there was no telephone in that room would Mr Summerfield please go and wake him?

A combination of natural disaster and hotel inefficiency – an unnerving thought in itself – struck Mr John Castles, from Lurgan, Northern Ireland, while on holiday on the Gulf Coast of Florida. A hurricane alert was broadcast over radio and TV, so he phoned reception to assure them that his family was packed and ready to move at a moment's notice, if so instructed. There was no further news, so the family carried on normally. They awoke on the Saturday morning to find the hotel surrounded by water and uprooted trees. On going down to reception, Mr Castles discovered all the guests and staff had deserted the hotel during the night, leaving his family alone to brave the elements. To make matters worse, the telephones were out of order, so they couldn't even ring home to say a final goodbye to their other children. Hours later, the manager reappeared to check on the damage. Far from being contrite, the manager reluctantly changed some of their dollar notes into coins and allowed them to buy some food – at their own expense – from the hotel's automatic food machines; a classic case of adding insult to injury.

The computer is the malevolent cause of many hotel horror-stories, particularly the epic saga of misunderstanding recounted by Mrs S. Romano, from Haifa, Israel.

A husband and wife, friends of Mrs Romano, were arriving in New York on different flights, but due at the same hotel. The computer got one vowel wrong on one of the names. The wife arrived first, checked in, and was told that her husband had not yet arrived, but would be sent up as soon as he appeared. Half an hour later, the man turned up, was checked into a different room, and told his wife had not yet arrived, but would be directed to his room when she appeared. For the next two days, they waited for their respective spouses, eventually calling a combination of airlines, hospitals, police stations and relations to find out where the other half was – and missing each other by minutes in the hotel restaurant. Eventually, they called home almost simultaneuously, to report to the children the depressing news that Mother/Father had vanished without trace. The children passed on the good news, and finally they were reunited, despite all the efforts of the hotel computer to keep them apart.

Sometimes, it seems, hotels deliberately spread confusion to keep the guests occupied, particularly if you judge by the strange things which appear in their brochures and notices. How else can one explain the notice in an Athens hotel, 'If this is your first visit, you are welcome to it'? Or the line in an Italian hotel brochure, 'we would very much like to have relations with you and will be most happy to dispose of all your clients'?

Wild Marketing Managers wouldn't drag me to the French hotel which advertised, 'Situated in the shadiest part of the town, you cannot fail to remark from the window the odours of the pine trees and our swimming pool.' Nor would I leave my wife unprotected in the place in Spain which assures visitors, 'If your wife needs something to do, she should apply to our suggestive Head Porter.'

All this, however, is Beginners' Starting Kit stuff. Venture further afield, to the wilder shores of hotel-keeping, and you take your life insurance in your hands.

'You are invited to visit our restaurant where you can eat the Middle East foods in an European ambulance,' proclaims the menu at an hotel in Ankara. And Michael Duffell, manager of the Ritz in London, swears he saw a notice in a Majorca hotel, 'On gala night, the chef throws his best dishes and all water used in cooking has been passed by the Manager personally.'

Even locking yourself in and phoning down for room service can have the most frightful results. 'If you wish for breakfast', promises a hotel in Madrid, 'Lift the telephone, ask for Room Service, and this will be enough for you to bring your food up.'

In one Istanbul hotel, you don't even have to bother with old-fashioned devices like the telephone. They have it all worked out: audio-visual effects, quadrophony, 3D, the lot. A sign on your bed reads, 'To call the Room Service, please to open door and call ROOM SERVICE!'

Packing your bags and escaping down the back stairs is no solution. An hotel in Naples forestalls guests doing a moonlight flit with this notice – in Italian only, be it noted – on its fire escape, 'This staircase is in a dangerous condition. It will be closed at the end of the tourist season.'

There was also no escape for the journalist, Barry Branford, when he checked into one of those Las Vegas hotels that charge rock-bottom rates, on the principle that they will clean up later by pressuring guests to spend money on their roulette wheels, gaming tables and fruit machines. Barry decided he could just about afford a fortnight, provided he resisted the temptation of pushing open the doors of the gambling saloon or pulling down the levers on the one-arm bandits. It took him exactly five minutes to discover the first catch. There were one-arm bandits everywhere in the hotel; behind the door of his room, in the bathroom, next to the bed, lined up in the restaurant, filling the lounge and bars, on parade along the corridors, even in the toilets. There was a more ominous second catch. There were men with broad shoulders and rearranged noses encouraging you to play them. The hotel, it turned out, was run by 'The Organis-

ation,' and Barry was worldly-wise enough to know that did
not mean the Young Men's Christian Association.

It soon became clear to the heavies that Barry was evading
his social responsibilities and two were deputed to follow
him around and steer him towards the machines. Whatever
they lacked in subtlety, nobody could accuse the two
torpedoes of failure to communicate. 'What's da madder?'
one enquired on the third day. 'You don't like da machines
or sump'n?'

As the fortnight dragged on, and the disapproval of the
thwarted management became more obvious, Barry began to
feel like a criminal on the run. Finally, in desperation, he put
on his swimsuit and went down to the hotel pool. But the
machines were there, lining the side like robot sunbathers

and almost outnumbering the customers. At least, he thought, there was one place they couldn't threaten him . . . and he dived into the water. As he surfaced in the middle, away from everyone, he was shattered to see the two heavies swimming doggedly towards him, pushing a cork raft ahead of them. On it was a fruit machine.

The hotel which is still in the cement-mixer used to be a stock joke in the bad old days of the package tour industry, when holidaymakers arrived at their resort to discover that their hotel consisted only of a hole in the ground and a hoarding bearing a colourful 'artist's impression' of the building-to-be.

You can imagine, then, the consternation among a party of VIPs who booked into the Sidi Dris Hotel, at Matmata, in Tunisia, and found themselves dumped in the middle of the desert with only a few sand dunes and a clump of palm trees for company.

There wasn't a building in sight, least of all the hotel they had been promised, yet the Sidi Dris had been in all the Tunisian guide books for years. As the group shuffled forward, hot, lost and confused, they almost tumbled over the lip of a large crater. And there below them, sticking out of the side, was a notice which plainly said, 'Hotel'. It was not a mirage. They had almost literally fallen into one of the world's most bizarre hotels. The Sidi Dris is an underground honeycomb of caves, tunnels and craters, all hollowed-out from the sandstone. The bedrooms are reached by rope ladder or steps cut into the rock. The rest of Matmata is the same, a troglodyte village where the 700 inhabitants bustle about below ground in a vast human rabbit-warren.

If you have ever wondered how prehistoric cavemen lived – plus a few mod. cons. – the Sidi Dris is your place. Or as one of the VIPs wrote on a postcard home, 'You must drop into our hotel. It's an absolute hole.'

Shocked Paws

You would think that being served with 'diced cat covered in rich sauce' at a banquet in Canton would put the tin hat on any further conversation. But Mr Peter Potter, of Antrobus, Cheshire, in China on a business trip, was made of sterner stuff. After congratulating his hosts on the dish, he told them his wife bred Burmese cats. What did she do with them? asked the Chinese. 'She sells them.' How much for? 'Oh, about £45 each.' There was a long pause as normally inscrutable faces registered every kind of astonishment, then the Chinese chorused, 'They must taste delicious!'

Living Dangerously

When, in April 1986, a guard on top of the Empire State Building in New York saw two men climbing over the safety fence, he shouted, 'Get off there!' They did, but not in the way he expected. The two men, Michael McCarthy and Alisdair Boyd, both visitors from Britain, jumped head first into thin air and parachuted 1,050 feet to the ground. Michael and Alisdair had hidden the parachutes under their raincoats on their way up the 102–story tower, after buying ordinary $3 entrance tickets.

They jumped, they said, because life was humdrum and nobody had ever done it before. All good things come to an end and, although Alisdair managed to hail a taxi and get away when he landed, Michael found himself snagged on a traffic light flashing, somewhat incongruously, the signal 'WALK. DON'T WALK.' He was later charged with 'public endangerment' and 'parachuting within city limits', which almost sound like offences specially made up for the occasion.

Alisdair and Michael were in good company. The world is full of eccentric travellers determined to get from Point A to Point B in the most dangerous, difficult or preposterous manner.

An Italian, Georgio Amoretti, flew over the Sahara and part of Alaska strapped to a kite, but they were only dummy runs for his attempt to cross the Atlantic in a car. Or rather, on a car. Amoretti had a Volkswagen Beetle stripped of its seats and filled with expanded polystyrene for buoyancy. Sitting on the roof, he put to sea at Las Palmas, in the Canary Islands, only to be rescued a few miles out.

In 1980, Jaromir Wagner, a Czech living in West Germany, succeeded in crossing the Atlantic by strapping himself to a pylon on top of an aircraft. The flight from Frankfurt to New York took 12 days and involved seven stops. To protect himself from temperatures as low as −70°C, Wagner wore thermal underwear, a wetsuit, a ski outfit, a leather suit, numerous woollen jumpers and a crash helmet. 'All the same,' he said at the end, 'I felt as though I was wearing little more than a swimming costume.'

After that, Sgt Walter Robinson's feat in 'walking' from Dover to Cap Gris Nez in 1978 on a home-made water shoe sounds almost humdrum. Larry Walters, a truck driver from Long Beach, California, is more in the grand tradition of loopy travellers. Larry launched himself into space, sitting in a sun-lounger harnessed to forty-five helium-filled meteorological balloons. Originally, he did not plan to go higher than 6,000 feet but the safety rope tethering him to the ground unexpectedly snapped and he shot up 15,000 feet into the airlanes of passing jumbo jets, some of whose pilots decided, there and then, to take early retirement.

Anxious to return to the safety of his garden, Larry tried shooting at the balloons with an airgun, with the result that he descended at high speed on to some power lines, temporarily plunging a section of Long Beach into darkness. By now the Federal Aviation Authority was eager to chat to him, though it took five months to work out the charges, which included 'operating a civil aircraft without an air-worthiness certificate, failing to maintain communication with a control tower and creating a traffic hazard'.

A sense of direction, surprisingly, is not a prime qualification for being an intrepid traveller. When Henry Weston started his epic 'jog round the world' at Tower Bridge, London, on April Fool's Day, 1984, he promptly got lost down the Old Kent Road. Dodging the TV cameras, he ducked into a launderette and whispered to two old ladies, 'Don't tell anyone you've seen me, but where is Dartford?' They drew him a map on the back of a cigarette packet and, encouraged by this, he asked them, 'Right. Where's Cairo?' Twenty-one months later, Weston was still jogging, having survived dysentery, ringworm, false arrest for bank robbery, a mugging in Melbourne, marauding monkeys, hijacking a glass-bottomed tourist boat out of Jordan, five collisions with cars and one with a a working elephant. 'I hate running, really,' he said when he arrived in Australia after an estimated 12,000 miles on the road. 'But all you can do is carry on. Sometimes I say it is the challenge, but actually I haven't a clue.'

Joseph Wolff, the son of a Bohemian rabbi who became a Christian convert and proselytiser, certainly knew exactly what impelled him to walk 600 miles across the Hindu Kush in the 1830s. It was to preach Christianity to the Jews of Turkestan, regarded by some people as the 'Lost Tribe of Israel'. It was the manner in which he travelled that was unusual. Completely naked.

In Reel Terms . . .

An American tourist who had spent 30 fruitless days on a salmon-fishing trip to Ireland was finally successful on the last day of his holiday. According to the *Daily Telegraph's* columnist, Peterborough, he showed his catch of one fish to the hotel barman and complained, somewhat bitterly, 'This damn' fish has cost me 700 dollars!' The barman shook his head sympathetically. 'Sure, and it's a good thing, then, that you didn't catch two,' he said.

Crash Course

Furious hooting, squealing brakes and shouts of abuse from foreign drivers on the Continent during 1986 may have been the result of a road safety campaign with the slogan 'Point a finger when you see a Wally,' organised by the West Midlands County Council. Their road safety committee distributed thousands of leaflets in a £12,000 contribution to European Road Safety Year, unaware that a captions mix-up might lead holidaying motorists on a short cut to the scrap-metal yard. The two signs given transposed captions were 'Give priority to oncoming vehicles' and 'End of no over-taking'; no comfort at all to a Frenchman coming the other way. Other, minor, mistakes involved readers being told they could drive too fast in Spain, and not fast enough through French towns and on Norwegian motorways. As the accusing finger of the Royal Society for the Prevention of Accidents pointed unerringly at the council, the chairman of the road safety committee commented glumly, 'I suppose people are saying we are the Wallies.'

Some People do have the Strangest Customs

I have been asked come pretty personal things in my time, but the question barked into my ear by the Customs officer at Sydney airport was intimate to a quite embarrassing degree. 'Are you,' he said menacingly, 'bringing in any semen?'

Frankly, I was not sure what was expected of me. Should I pipe up in a squeaky voice, 'Certainly not, saucy.' Or reply in a *basso profundo* 'What do *you* think?' The consequences of admitting outright that I, er, well, *suppose I was*, didn't bear further contemplation.

As the colour drained from my face, the Customs officer thrust in front of me a list of prohibited articles. The first one was 'Parrots', which in my nervous state I misread as Perrotts. Under 'S' for Semen, however, all was mercifully revealed. Frozen bull's sperm, for the purposes of artificial insemination of cattle, is forbidden. You will be as relieved to know that as I was.

Confrontation with Customs officers is the same the world over; you are on a hiding to nothing. The unrelenting zeal (to use a polite word) of the average Customs officer can be gauged by an incident when Sir Freddie Laker's airline collapsed a few years back. The news broke when one plane-load of Laker holidaymakers was halfway across Europe, bound for Majorca. The plane immediately turned back to the airport they had just left, where, having lost both their holidays and their money, the passengers were informed by Customs that they had to forfeit the Duty Frees they had bought on the way out, or pay the appropriate duty. The milk of human kindness is rarely encountered on such an epic scale.

Pop-singer Elton John came unstuck in Australia when he ambled up to the Customs desk at Sydney wearing a denim outfit covered in 150 sewn-on stickers and badges. The unsmiling officers singled out three of the badges and declared them 'offensive'. They laboriously 'censored' them with sticking plaster before allowing Elton to continue into the airport lounge.

A few years ago, when Spain still laboured under the puritanical rule of General Franco, I was standing in Malaga airport when a crowd of jolly package-tourists arrived from Luton. The group was waved through Customs in the customary languid Spanish manner, until one of the officers spotted a copy of *Playboy* peeking out of a passenger's flight bag. It was as if the Customs man had suddenly been confronted with anti-Christ. 'Feelth!' he spluttered, snatching at the magazine. 'Pornografia! Is not allowed in Espain!' With that, he furiously threw in into a corner.

Highly mortified, the holidaymaker slunk out, followed by his subdued companions. The doors had hardly swung shut behind them when all the Customs officers pounced on the magazine with shrieks of glee, shouting 'Mine!' 'Me first!' 'After you, Pedro!' It dawned upon me that this was not the first time they had played this little trick.

Cricket-enthusiast John Francis encountered the same kind of stunned disbelief when he tried to bring his cricket bat through a remote French Customs-post. They had never seen one before. Was it for hockey, they wondered, or for tennis?

Baseball, perhaps? Patiently, Mr Francis explained it was for cricket, adding a brief description of the game for good measure.

The Frenchmen shrugged in the dismissive way they have, handed Mr Francis a list of Customs duties at least a hundred pages long and suggested he find an appropriate category for his exotic import. Which is how Our Hero paid 1.25 francs duty on an *'engin sportif sans mouvement mecanique'*.

Thanks to Rome customs, American Express executive David Jarvis claims to be the only golfer who ever teed off with a trombone. Asked to explain what was in his padlocked golf bag, he replied, reasonably enough, 'Clubs'. The customs officer looked none the wiser, so Mr Jarvis demonstrated a classic golf swing, with impeccable follow-through. 'Ah,' said the customs man, 'trombone. There is no duty on musical instruments.' Not wishing to argue the point, Mr Jarvis nodded and checked through. Later on, he won his golf tournament; without anyone asking him to blow a tune on his Number Two Iron.

It is not often that a Customs officer has to eat his words, but it happened in Ireland when Mrs Jane Powell arrived at Dun Laoghaire with a parcel of aubergines she had bought at Harrods. 'Dem's roots,' said the officer with disapproving finality. 'You need an import licence to bring in roots. Colorado Beetle Act, an' all dat.'

There was no convincing the man. So Mrs Powell agreed to leave the aubergines behind, but told him not to destroy them. She then wrote to the Department of Agriculture explaining the misunderstanding and asking for an import licence.

Weeks dragged past, until a mimeographed reply arrived, *'A Chara!* Your application for an import licence to bring roots into this country, not having been made in the proper way, cannot be granted. *Mise le meas.* P.S., No licence is required in respect of aubergines.'

It was with some satisfaction that Mrs Powell returned to the Customs office to reclaim her legal vegetables; by now, brown, wrinkled and uneatable.

At least Mrs Powell didn't have to wolf them on the spot. Unlike Rhiannon Andrews, a PA for Thames Television's *Wish You Were Here?* holiday programme, who innocently tried to cross the Customs line at St Lucia with a banana in her flight bag.

St Lucia's main export is bananas. They grow wall-to-wall across the island and the entire economy depends on them. So they are a mite touchy about people bringing them in, even just one.

'Eat it!' commanded the scandalised Customs officer, before allowing the poor girl to cross the barrier. Rhiannon slowly skinned and ate the forbidden fruit and, with a supremely disdainful gesture, handed him the skin to throw away.

Trying to foresee what wierd and wonderful things are prohibited in each country is like entering an Alice in Wonderland world where the most innocent, everyday article is regarded as a danger to national security or a threat to public morals.

You can't send playing cards or potatoes to Fernando Po, ashtrays or macaroni to Afghanistan, worn clothes (unless disinfected) to Argentina, contraceptives to France, powdered cocoa beans to West Germany, Mexican jumping beans to India or carbon paper to Sri Lanka. You will come unstuck if you try to post chewing gum to the Soviet Republic of Kazakhstan and attempting to send high-flying carrier pigeons to East Germany – however beautifully gift-wrapped – will only result in your getting the bird.

As you stand there in the post office, being ceremonially stripped of chewing gum, jumping beans and carbon paper, do not expect any lucid explanation of why and wherefore. Particularly in Turkey, where the written Instruction for Customs Declarations only makes matters worse. Among the things you *can* bring in are:

Ready and conditioned wearing apparel for his use, printed matter for his reading and papers for his writing, articles for his playing and sport exercise, musical instruments which he knows how to play, quantity of food and drinks needed during his trip provided the articles are in compatabilness with his social position.

112

Passengers declaring any other effects, the notice continues, must declare them and 'pass through the door of the signal lamp'.

The subtlety and deviousness of the Instructions would have done credit to the old Ottoman Empire. For a start, how do you prove to a disbelieving Customs official that you know how to play a sitar, ocarina or contra-bassoon? Give a virtuoso recital of old Turkish airs and dances in the customs hall? And what kind of food and drink is compatible with your social status? Tinned truffles? A pound of Wall's sausages? If you were a Baronet, would a tin of spaghetti rings be confiscated as below your social level? Is a bottle of Bollinger too good for a plumber travelling Economy Class?

Fail to convince the Customs officer with your rendition of *Oh, for the Wings of a Dove* on a football referee's whistle, or try to smuggle a saveloy through in your executive briefcase, and the penalties could be horrific. No less than a one-way passage through the dreaded door of the signal lamp, from whence no traveller returns.

Do not think that waving H.M. passport and mouthing all that imperial rubbish about 'without let or hindrance' will

get you out of trouble. Frankly, passports are not worth the paper they are stamped on.

Ask Mrs Patricia Layen, of Sutton Coldfield, whose husband went abroad on business, taking her passport by mistake. The gender-bending passport was scrutinised several times but nobody seemed to notice that Patricia Layen had not merely changed sex, but sprouted silver hair and black, bushy eyebrows.

Applying for a Spanish passport, a colleague was asked to supply four photographs 'frontal and uncovered' and another friend travels on an Egyptian passport which, under 'distinguishing marks', has the official entry, 'Appendix scar on bridge of nose'. If you are a woman, let me give you one word of advice: don't ever go to Cairo for a nose-bob operation. You could end up with a revolutionary transplant.

Even with sanctuary in sight, your knuckles chalk-white on the luggage trolley and the Customs bench safely behind, you could still be pipped at the post. A *Daily Telegraph* correspondent was just about to clear Jan Smuts airport in Johannesburg – noted for its charmless welcome – when the last Customs officer in the row stopped him. The writer thought he heard the man say, in a thick Afrikaans accent, 'Now strip!' As the furious *Telegraph* man began to remove his shirt and tie, the South African grimaced and shouted, 'Ah sid, 'ave a nawice trep!'

As I said; a hiding to nothing.

A Load on One's Mind

A British ski party travelling by coach from Newcastle to the slopes of La Mongie – in the French Pyrenees and near the main route to the pilgrimage centre of Lourdes – were mystified when their driver landed them a hundred miles off course and well on the way to the Spanish frontier. Rapid consultation of the map revealed that the Geordie driver had faithfully followed road signs all the way which said *'Poids Lourds'* [Heavy vehicles].

Call of the Wild

All the remote Australian village of Eucla was famous for was a swearing parrot, the most inhospitable pub in the country – with notices reading 'Don't bring your own food', 'Don't ask for water' and 'No cheques cashed' – and eighty inhabitants who spent the evenings drinking and swapping tall stories. That was until the Topless Nature Girl of the Nullabor Plain bounded into view, her hair streaming in the wind and leading a herd of red kangaroos.

It all started with a rabbit-trapper, who staggered into the curmudgeonly pub one morning, babbling about seeing the half-naked Nature Girl in the desert feeding a kangaroo in the dawn light. The drinkers were agog, none more so than a tourist from Perth, Western Australia, named Geoff Pearce, who went straight to the telephone and sold the 'story' to a news agency.

As the yarn appeared in newspapers and magazines all over the world, the Eucla drinkers gladly supplied more details. Some of the desert bushmen, they said, had seen the wild girl dressed only in a kangaroo-skin skirt and leading her flock. Only a few days earlier, a party of bushmen had tried to capture her, but she escaped into the bush. However, they had tracked down her lair and were sure they could seize her. It was not long before the drinkers were spending all day answering the pub telephone. The calls came from distraught newspapers in three continents. The German magazine *Stern* offered a small fortune for interviews and pictures and the BBC, it was rumoured, intended to divert a *World About Us* camera crew – already in Australia – to Nullabor Plain in an attempt to track down the Nature Girl.

With the attention of the world focussed on Eucla, the girl suddenly vanished, never to be seen again. A year later, the truth came out when the original rabbit-trapper admitted, 'Actually I never saw the Nature Girl myself, but the story had been going round the district for about eight months, so

I assumed it was true.' The whole thing had been a hoax and Eucla is still famous for nothing, except that the locals now have a lot more to laugh about in the pub that refuses to serve water.

Lapse of Mammary

Engaging in intelligent conversation with one's fellow passenger on a long flight is not so easy, as Mr H. H. Coutts, an executive of Shell Research, found out to his acute mortification. Travelling to Guatemala City, Mr Coutts found conversation limited by the fact that he spoke little Spanish, and the man in the next seat less English. However, Mr Coutts was encouraged when the man turned from gazing out of

the window and exlaimed, 'I'm a tit man!' Mr Coutts replied
jovially, 'So am I.' Puzzled, the man pointed out of the
window and repeated, more slowly, 'Amatitlan', the name
of the lakeside town over which they were passing. Further
conversation, Mr Coutts recalled later, was carried on in
monosyllables. There was a happy ending to Mr Coutts's
embarrassing experience. In a magazine competition to find
the most amusing travel story, he deservedly won first prize.
No, not a return flight to Guatemala, but a holiday for two
in Egypt – Mr Coutts no doubt exercising caution this time
in any reference to Nefertiti.

Time Bomb

Readers of Belfast's Irish-language daily newspaper *L'a* had
a lot of trouble with holiday dates in 1986. A calendar
published by the paper had March beginning on a Monday
instead of Saturday and cropped to only thirty days. The lost
day was transferred to September, which had thirty-one days
instead of thirty. October also lost a day, which was made
up for by an extra one being tacked on to November.
Emerging from total disorientation, readers faced another
obstacle at Christmas time. The calendar made Christmas
Day Tuesday instead of Thursday, ushering in Hogmanay
two days earlier than the rest of Britain. One way and
another, it was a relief to get to 1987.

The Voyeur now Standing at Platform Three

Gad, sir, it is bad enough your ordinary, everyday commuter
being late for work because his train was delayed, but when

it happens to the Queen; I mean, no wonder we lost the Empire. The Queen's interminable ride on the Fenman Express from Sandringham to London, early in 1986, was not exactly a public relations triumph. Her Majesty arrived an hour late, distinctly unamused, leaving mass egg-on-face at British Rail.

The Royal Family had hardly recovered from the *lèse majesté* of it all when it was revealed in the House of Commons that another member, said to be the Duchess of Kent, had been disturbed by 'shocking noises' coming from an adjoining compartment on the same train. Unable to endure any longer the 'grunts, groans, scrapings and bangings', the Royal complained to a ticket-inspector, who went to investigate. The neighbouring compartment had its shutters down, so the inspector slid open the door. He discovered a naked couple 'dressed only in a First Class ticket' and engaged in what *The Sun* newspaper might have described as 'a torrid afternoon of uninhibited passion'.

As any aged commuter will tell you at the drop of a ticket-inspector's hat, none of this would have happened in the 'good old days' of rail travel. Could you imagine the cream-and-brown carriages of the Great Western Railway, like flying Mars-bars, depositing the Monarch one second late at Cardiff? Or the Flying Scotsman calling it a day at Crewe, amid shouts of 'ALL change! And that means YOU!'?

A nation's entire credibility rested on the punctuality of its trains. Wasn't that our great bequest to India? Didn't Mussolini boost Italy's international status overnight by making the trains run on time? And as for the nude frolics on the Fenman Express (or should it now be renamed the Funman Express?), people in those days actually dressed up to go on train journeys, not the other way round.

Alas for misplaced nostalgia. The fact is that the early days of rail in Britain were fraught with disaster. Buying a rail ticket was tantamount to taking your life in your hands, and only the most optimistic traveller invested in a return. Carriages were infested with thieves, con-men and black-mailers. On one day alone, in 1848, Eastern Counties Railway passengers lost 76 items of luggage to assorted robbers. The higher your social status, the more you lost. The Countess of Dudley had her family jewels, then worth more than £50,000, stolen at Paddington Station. They were never recovered.

In 1854, an American tourist wrote to the *Derby Mercury*, 'I am not a timid man, but I never enter an English railway carriage without having in my pocket a loaded revolver. How am I to know my travelling companion is not a madman escaped from confinement, or a runaway criminal?' Dangerously barmy fellow-passengers were obviously a big problem. 'It is not soothing to the nerves', wrote the railway historian, John Pendleton, 'to travel on the railway with a powerful lunatic, who insists, drawing an ugly clasp-knife, that you tell him the names of all the stations the train is passing. It is so terrifying that you would be wise to escape from the compartment, creep along the footboard and seek refuge in the guard's van.'

Talking about creeping along the footboard brings one, quite naturally, to Peeping Toms and torrid afternoons of uninhibited passion. In 1890, a Birmingham inquest heard how a railwayman had been swept to his death from the side of a train while spying on a 'courting couple' in the next-door compartment. Apparently, he had inched along the footboard to sneak a look at what the court delicately referred to as 'their movements'. The coroner was told that this practice was 'quite common among railway servants'.

But what about disconcerted monarchs? I hear you ask. Ten a penny. A train on which Queen Victoria was travelling jolted and shook so dangerously that she ordered it to be stopped at Wigan. There, her devoted servant John Brown was sent directly to the railway superintendent with a message from Her Majesty. 'The Queen', he reported, 'says her carriage is shaking like the Devil.'

Things had not improved by the reign of Edward VII. In 1890, the then Prince of Wales burst from a train, complaining furiously about a sheet of fine black dust which had covered his saloon table and all the dresses of the ladies in his party.

The dust, it turned out, had percolated through a new-fangled ventilator the railway company had fitted specially for the journey. Public relations comes a cropper again.

The Prince was lucky not to bump into an ordinary member of the railway staff. Then as now, porters and guards were renowned for their rudeness. A letter-writer to *The Times* described 'an incident at Ilford' when he opened the carriage door, got down and waited for his wife and child to follow. But before the couple could make a move, the guard slammed the door shut and signalled the train away. Distraught mother and howling child were carried to Romford, five miles further on, where the woman was ordered to pay the extra fare. 'Are the public', asked the husband, not unreasonably, 'to be dragged about wherever the railway company chooses?'

Hiccups, breakdowns and diversions were a daily routine, part of the thrill of travel. One of the reasons was that loco-motive staff were often hopelessly incompetent. An optician complained in *The Times* that he had met an engine-driver who could not tell red from green and a signalman was discovered to have one poor eye, and the other capable of seeing no further than twelve inches.

Not surprisingly, the railways echoed to the sound of rending metal. When railwayman Tom Walsh spotted Loco-motive No. 76 clanking furtively along the line at Pulbor-ough, Sussex, he realised something was wrong. It was not just the three sets of splintered level-crossing gates festooning the buffers that aroused his suspicions. There was also no engine-driver. Like a cowboy vaulting a runaway horse, Walsh leaped aboard, turned off the steam and the eighteen-mile joyride of Locomotive No. 76 hissed to an end. How had the engine escaped? The sorry tale came out at the enquiry. A cleaner in the shed at Petworth had left No. 76 for a few moments with her steam up. He had also left her in forward gear, and with her steam regulator open. Any self-respecting loco would have done the same; she made a dash for it.

That was in 1859, but Locomotive No. 76's bid for freedom was by no means unique. In 1871, a runaway engine shot out of Pontypool Road station on a wild nine-mile ride in which she demolished seventeen sets of level crossing gates. Luckily, it was Sunday, and being Wales, nobody was around to get hurt.

The most destructive rampage occurred on the Somerset & Dorset Joint Railway's line between Radstock and Wellow, when a rogue engine escaped at fifty miles an hour, pushing eight waggons before it. Terrified railmen ran for their lives as the train hurtled through stations and level crossings.

At Midford, where the double track changed to a single line, there was chaos. 'Signals and telegraph poles fell like ninepins,' wrote an observer.

A signalman's cabin collapsed under his feet as one waggon demolished its masonry base, six waggons shot one after another over an embankment and for a distance of three hundred yards the line was littered with debris. Yet, although the track was damaged, the locomotive continued at unabated speed, pushing before her like a handcart the remnant of one waggon running on two wheels only.

This wondrous Buster Keaton comedy ended when a door dropped from the waggon and fell under the wheels of the locomotive, sending it thundering off the rails. Now, why can't our new high speed train go like *that?*

In those days railway stations tended to be manned either by old buffers or tender youths. After one mishap it was discovered that a busy stretch of line had been left in the charge of a seventeen-year-old lad who could neither read nor write, was too weak to pull all the signal levers and had run out of paraffin for the warning lamps.

Even among trained railwaymen, routine discipline was haphazard, to say the least. In 1873 two trains were waiting to move off on a dangerous bend at Menheniot in Cornwall. 'Right away, Dick!' the signalman shouted to one of the drivers as he got the all clear signal. Unhappily, he had forgotten one important point. Both drivers were named Dick. To the signalman's dismay, both trains shot off. A few miles up the track, they met each other again at full speed. The miracle was that there were not more crashes.

Favoured individuals were often given trains to themselves
– real-life Hornby train sets to play with – in which they
roamed the railways conducting obscure experiments. These
trains steamed into view at the most unexpected and incon-
venient moments. in 1838 an engine driven by a blithely
incompetent rail enthusiast named Dr Dionysius Lardner was
involved in two collisions before it was finally ordered off
the Great Western line. The bridge-builder Isambard Brunel
thought nothing of commandeering a spare engine when late
for an appointment, rather on the lines of hailing a taxi. Once
he drove himself from Bristol to London at fifty miles an
hour on the wrong track. When asked what he would have
done if he had met a train coming the opposite way, he
replied aggressively, 'I would have driven it off the line, sir!'
Engineers would take an engine from its shed as casually as
an Oxford student would jump on a bike. If a train was late,
they would go out to meet it. One driver wrote, 'Many times
I've gone out to look for a late train that was expected, and
many times I've seen the train coming and reversed the
engine and run back out of its way as quickly as I could.'

Engine maintenance was a rough and ready affair. When
a locomotive found a hill particularly hard going, the fireman
would drop a ball of tallow down the blast pipe to lubricate
the cylinders. It was common practice to pop in one of these
pep-pills while the train was chugging along, with the
fireman crawling along the running-plate to open the
smokebox door.

If a train broke down, the driver merely got the local bobby
to stand in the middle of the track with his hand raised to
warn oncoming traffic. Alternately, the crew could light a
warning bonfire between the rails. The only thing to
remember was not to combine the two.

Travelling by trains was a perilous business in every way;
the only time you were safe was when you were at a stand-
still. Drivers used to screw down the safety valves to obtain
greater steam pressure going up hills. Signals – the early
ones were like sails – blew away in high winds. Boilers were

inclined to blow up. Even time itself became meaningless, as each station observed its own 'local time', and it was theoretically possible to arrive in one station before you had left the previous one – a fact which would have delighted Albert Einstein. In 1849, after a spot of timetable confusion on the East Lancashire Railway, the culprit was found to be the clock at Bootle station, which, according to one witness, 'went wildly'.

There was, however, one group of people even more fool-hardy than the railwaymen themselves – the passengers. Trains were a wonderful novelty and passengers had no idea of the dangers involved in high speed travel, or even low speed travel. Many passengers ended up in hospital after leaping from moving trains to rescue hats, gloves or news-papers. Occasionally, anxious porters would lock them in their compartments for their own safety.

Accustomed to riding on stagecoaches, some travellers insisted on squatting on the roofs of the carriages to admire the passing view. One train was held up for hours because they refused to come down, and they were finally manhandled into sheep trucks. Roof travelling only lost its allure after hundreds of passengers had lost their footing and been scattered along the line like litter, or swept off by low bridges they didn't see coming.

The romance of rail? It is a diverting thought, but completely on the wrong lines. The trouble with nostalgia is that it is like trying to drive along a motorway while gazing fondly at the rear-view mirror; no future in it. Taking every-thing into account, the Queen was lucky to get to her desti-nation at all. At least she didn't get shaken like a maracca, lose the Crown Jewels or end up covered in soot. Not to speak of the embarrassment of overhearing torrid afternoons of uninhibited passion. In the end, there is something to be said for low technology.

Phew, What a Scorcher

The story about the tourist in India who left his suede shoes outside his bedroom door, merely for brushing, and found them scraped down to the bare leather and brilliantly polished, is probably apocryphal. But Mr Jack Harding, of Dartford, Kent, found scorch marks on the cuff of his suit after it had come back from the hotel cleaners. He remonstrated with the manager, who assured him the marks could be removed. Three days later, just as Mr Harding was due to leave on an early flight, the suit was returned minus the marks. Later that day, in Kathmandu, Mr Harding unfolded his suit for a business meeting . . . to find one arm four inches shorter than the other. What the manager hadn't told him was that the marks could be removed by snipping six inches off the sleeve.

Bedtime Story

For a secretary or personal assistant, going away with the boss on a business trip can be a harassing experience. Too often, the boss expects services which were never in the written contract. A glamorous editorial assistant on the British Printing Corporation accompanied her boss on a trip to the Frankfurt Book Fair. Determined to keep the relationship on a strictly business level, she made sure that their adjoining hotel rooms did not have a communicating door. On her first evening, having made all the appropriate excuses about being tired and needing a good night's rest, she collapsed thankfully into her own bed just before midnight.

It was one of those vaguely kinky German massage-beds which vibrate when you put a mark or two into a slot. At 3 a.m., a coin which had been lodged in the machinery dropped into place, setting the whole apparatus in motion. For ten minutes, despite every effort to stop it, the bed thumped loudly and rhythmically against the wall separating the two rooms. Nothing was mentioned about the strange noises in the night when the girl met her boss at breakfast in the morning. But the look on his face said it all.

Not the Right Type

The most glorious misprints are those in which the alteration of a single letter causes total devastation. Mr Ashley Courtenay, the nonagenerian publisher of the 'Let's Halt Awhile' hotel guides, was mortified when he spotted a misprint in one edition which referred to guests 'happily starving' at an hotel, instead of 'happily staying'. In the following edition, he made a point of double-checking the entry. It was correct. But in the following line, the same hotel was now described as 'a particularly peaceful hovel'.

No Show

Even the most loyal resident of Cairns, the semi-tropical township on the edge of Australia's Great Barrier Reef, would admit that its cultural achievements were, well, modest. So it came as a surprise when an American tourist stepped from the inaugural Qantas flight from Los Angeles to the newly built Cairns international airport, and started enquiring about the films to be seen at the festival. Since there is only one cinema in Cairns, whose programmes, to say the least, are intellectually undemanding, there was a lot of head-scratching. 'You must have heard of the Cairns international film festival?', the American kept repeating, with increasing desperation. Discreet enquiries at Quantas unearthed the truth. The American thought he had booked for Cannes.

How to Cable Home that the Ship's Captain Has Gone Mad and the Crew Has Run Amok

Years ago, in my far-off schooldays, my careers master tried valiantly to steer me in the direction of a shipping office. Not a chance. I scoffed at the idea of spending all my life knee deep in manifests, estimates of cargo by metric volume and bills of lading. It all seemed a short cut to terminal boredom.

It was only when I chanced on an old copy of the *ABC Universal Telegraphic Code* that I was overcome with the full realisation of what I had missed. One glance at the section devoted to shipping opened up a thrilling world of stricken vessels, mountainous waves, perilous ports of call, resourceful captains, mutinous crews, awful dangers and miraculous rescues. All this could have been mine.

In a single word, the Code could conjure up a scene as dramatic as anything in *The Cruel Sea*. Just picture it. One of your company's cargo ships has run aground in the South Atlantic. Water is pouring in, Argentinian pirates have looted everything of value, the captain has bolted and – as if all this is not enough to send any company accountant to an early grave – the vessel is beginning to break up. As you survey the doleful scene, mentally writing off a couple of million pounds with the barest twitch of an eyebrow, you suddenly spot the opportunity for saving a few pence on the final bill. There, in the *Universal Code*, is a word which means, 'The vessel found on examination to have sustained so much damage as not to be worth the cost of getting her off; the operations have therefore been stopped and it is now intended to move all equipment from the vessel.' Without hesitation, you cable the codeword EAUZH. The company may have consigned ten years' cash flow to Davy Jones's locker but, with messages costing £1 a word from some benighted cable-office in the Falklands, you have saved your firm all of £39 – a coup which might earn you a carillon in your honour on the Lutine Bell at Lloyds.

Whatever the crisis or catastrophe, the *Universal Code* had, and for all I know still has, a word for it. Holiday disasters and travel fiascos are meat and drink to the compilers.

Tap out the signal AWHOU on your Morse transmitter and it means, 'captain apparently insane'. Had a copy of the Code been lying around the *Bounty* in 1789, the whole course of history would have been changed and Hollywood would have been three films the poorer.

Captains are apparently a constant source of worry for shipping lines, for there are codewords for 'captain lost overboard', 'captain not to be found', captain refused to go to sea', 'Arrest the captain', captain arrested' and 'Send another captain'. The romance of it all! Give that lot to Joseph Conrad and he would have churned out another 500,000–word novel of adventure on the high seas before you could say EATUH ('Captain and crew arrested for smuggling').

If there is one thing more unreliable than your average captain, however, it is the crew. To receive the codeword for 'crew are all drunk' is an ominous enough start to any

voyage, but there could be far worse trouble ahead. In escalating order of alarm, the *Universal Code* has 'crew before the Consul', 'crew down with scurvy', 'crew have mutinied', 'crew have deserted', 'crew alleging vessel unseaworthy', 'Native crew running amok' and the despairing, 'Can do nothing with crew'.

It is then that the captain, assuming he is not lost overboard, insane or arrested, can exact the supreme penalty. It is with bowed shoulders and a heavy heart that he cables the dreaded ETSUX, for 'May I execute at own discretion?' No managing director, safe at home, can shoulder a more grave and onerous burden than having to decide whether to inflict the final punishment. A lesser man might flinch from such responsibility, but putting on the Black Cap and muttering 'The Lord have mercy on your souls', the MD transmits the dolorous signal, 'Do best to execute.'

The world of Fleet Street newspapers may not have the same power of life and death, but when it comes to brevity, the Press can maybe teach the *Universal Code* a thing or two. And without even resorting to enigmatic codewords.

Over the years, parsimonious foreign editors have instilled into far-flung and feckless correspondents the necessity for keeping messages as short as possible. When Sir David English was Foreign Editor of the *Daily Express*, it is said, he rebuked a dilatory correspondent with a cable that combined the minimum amount of words with the maximum of menace, 'UPPULL SOCKS QUICKMOST OR UNJOB'.

One of newspaperland's most unlikely correspondents was the novelist Evelyn Waugh, who was sent by the *Daily Mail* in a moment of mental aberration to cover the war in Abyssinia. His first effort came to grief. Anxious to disguise a 'scoop' from his fellow Pressmen, he cabled his story to London in Latin. It would have undoubtedly made the front page, except for one unforeseen obstacle – nobody at the *Mail* understood Latin. The story was 'spiked'. Waugh was not much luckier with his next report. The office had got wind of a story, almost certainly false, that an English nurse had been killed in a hospital explosion at Adowa. They sent Waugh an urgent cable, 'NEED SOONMOST LIFE STORY NURSE UPBLOWN ADOWA.' Try as he could, Waugh could not track down the hospital, least of all the nurse. Sensing that the whole thing was a wild goose chase, he shot back the truculent message, 'NURSE UNUPBLOWN ADOWA'.

For many correspondents, foreign travel provides a splendid excuse for cabling laconic messages back to their editors. Though few have succeeded in being as droll as the humorist, Robert Benchley, who wired back to his office from Venice, 'STREETS FULL OF WATER. PLEASE ADVISE'. A *Time* magazine reporter, who had been sent to cover a story aboard an aircraft carrier in the Pacific, wired back his expenses at the end of the assignment. The bill got as far as the office accountant, who cabled him succinctly, but with that accusatory tone beloved of accountants, 'EXPLAIN CHARGES FOR TAXIS'. The reporter promptly cabled back, 'BIG CARRIER'. Occasionally, editors get their own back, as in the crisp exchange between a reporter and his irascible

boss after he had been sent at great cost to cover a disastrous flood in America. Striving for the apocalyptic touch, the reporter started his story with the words, 'GOD LOOKS DOWN ON A SCENE OF TOTAL DEVASTATION TONIGHT AS . . .' Even before the sentence was finished, the editor was through on another line. 'FORGET FLOOD', wired the editor, 'INTERVIEW GOD'.

Dialling the Almighty was a lot easier on the old *Daily Express*. The proprietor, the Bible-quoting Lord Beaverbrook, was considered to have a direct line to God, but even he could sometimes get his lines crossed. In those mischievous days, a *Daily Express* Editor always knew when the Beaver had the skids under him. He was sent on a world cruise at the newspaper's expense. By the time he returned, another editor was safely installed in his office and the pay-off cheque was waiting on the doormat. The Beaver once capriciously sent an erring editor on the slow boat to nowhere without first deciding who the successor might be. When the editor's boat reappeared on the horizon, they still had not found a replacement. Frantically, the Beaver cabled the editor, 'GO ROUND AGAIN!'

Alas and alack, with the demise of the GPO's telegram service, the witty and ingenious cable-writers have been cut short in mid-sentence. No floral-bordered 'Telemessage' can have quite the same tone as the lofty message received by the Lord of the Manor at Rumwell Hall, Taunton, the day before the outbreak of World War Two: 'NO HUNTING IF ENGLAND DECLARES WAR. TUCKER, MASTER OF HOUNDS'. And certainly no telephone call, however convincing, would ever have the galvanic effect on the twelve people who once received the hoax message from a friend, 'ALL IS DISCOVERED. FLY AT ONCE.' Nine of them immediately took the next plane to France.

Horse Sense

Travelling abroad for the BBC involves, among many other talents, the financial acumen of a trained accountant, if only to make sense of the Corporation's tortuous expense-account regulations. One rule is that any item purchased on expenses automatically becomes the property of the BBC and must be accounted for. The late Sir Huw Wheldon recalled how the wildlife expert, David Attenborough, returned from some gruelling trek through the rain-forests of Ecuador with an expense-sheet of daunting length and complexity. With unerring aim, Sir Huw homed in on an item which read 'To purchase of packhorses, £40'. His sense of corporate responsibility fully aroused, Sir Huw searched for some clue that the horses had later been sold and the money refunded. Maybe David Attenborough had followed BBC regulations to the letter and arranged for them to be crated and returned to Lime Grove studios. Or could it be that the animals were being pampered in some outrageously exppnsive stables in Quito, to be paid for in perpetuity by the Corporation? Thoroughly alarmed at the possibilities, Sir Huw scanned the neatly typewritten sheets until he came to the word 'Pack-horses', followed by an asterisk. It was with enormous relief that he read at the bottom of the page, 'Horses eaten by natives'. 'I knew then', said Sir Huw later, 'that David had all the makings of a great administrator.' Sir Huw's assessment was remarkably astute, for in 1969 David Attenborough was appointed Director of Programmes.

Wish You Were Here?

Some of the most distinguished victims of Nazi persecution ended up in Hollywood and frequently met to chat about old times, the conversation often turning to memorable holidays of the past. The Hungarian playwright, Odon von Horvath, was once describing his hiking experiences in the Alps to Bertolt Brecht, the left-wing author of *The Threepenny Opera*. On one walk, well off the beaten track and just after the snows had melted, he had stumbled on the fully-clothed skeleton of a young man, with a rucksack on his back. Inside the rucksack was a postcard, addressed to the man's family, saying, 'Having a wonderful time.'

'How terrible,' said Brecht, 'What did you do?'

'Posted it,' said von Horvath.

Warm Welcome

Like many immigrants to Britain, Mohammed Ajeeb under-
estimated the severity of our winter. It was a raw and foggy
day in November, 1957, when eighteen-year-old Mr Ajeeb
flew in to Heathrow from Pakistan, dressed in a light shirt
and inadequately thin suit. At St Pancras Station he bought
a ticket for Nottingham and sat in the icy carriage, shivering
uncontrollably and dreading the journey ahead. Then a
stranger entered, and immediately took pity on him. He
switched on the heating, put his overcoat across Mr Ajeeb's
knees and brought him a cup of cocoa from the platform
trolley. The Good Samaritan identified himself as a farmer
and suggested Mr Ajeeb give him a call if he ever needed a
job. But Mr Ajeeb had to leave at Nottingham, where the
stranger ordered a taxi for him.

Thirty years passed and Mr Ajeeb became a successful
buisnessman and, eventually, Britain's first Asian mayor.
However, he never forgot the incident and on his first day
as Lord Mayor of Bradford he appealed for help in tracing
the stranger on the train. Some friends showed him pictures
taken in the 1950s of the late Ted Moult, the farmer and TV
personality, and Mr Ajeeb recognised him as the man.

At a civic reception in honour of Mr Moult, at Bradford
City Hall, Mr Ajeeb said, 'It is very important that I have
this opportunity to say thank you after all these years. It was
spontaneous kindness and Mr Moult gave help without my
asking. Since then, I have faced discrimination and have been
abused and insulted because of my race, but I have never
forgotten him. He gave me all the comfort I needed for that
first journey.' Then the two men drank a toast . . . in cocoa.